Platonic Jung
And the Nature of Self

Jane Weldon

CHIRON PUBLICATIONS • ASHEVILLE, NORTH CAROLINA

www.ChironPublicatons.com

Interior and cover design by Danijela Mijailovic.
Printed primarily in the United States of America.

ISBN 978-1-63051-401-3 paperback
ISBN 978-1-63051-402-0 hardcover
ISBN 978-1-63051-403-7 electronic

Library of Congress Cataloging-in-Publication Data

Names: Weldon, Jane, 1958- author.
Title: Platonic Jung / by Jane Weldon.
Description: Asheville, North Carolina : Chiron Publications, [2017] | Includes bibliographical references and index.
Identifiers: LCCN 2017004744 (print) | LCCN 2017017138 (ebook) | ISBN 9781630514037 (E-book) | ISBN 9781630514013 (pbk. : alk. paper) | ISBN 9781630514020 (hardcover : alk. paper)
Subjects: LCSH: Jung, C. G. (Carl Gustav), 1875-1961. | Plato. | Jungian psychology. | Psychoanalysis and philosophy.
Classification: LCC BF109.J8 (ebook) | LCC BF109.J8 W45 2017 (print) | DDC 150.19/54092--dc23
LC record available at https://lccn.loc.gov/2017004744

I dedicate this work to the Divine Mystery at the heart of all Being,
And
To Plato and Jung, in whose company I have gotten
closer to that mystery.

Acknowledgements

My deepest gratitude is for the presence in my soul that called me to this project and remained my best guide.

I want to thank my readers who spent time on the book in the midst of their busy lives. Deldon McNeely, Jungian Analyst, read the whole book several times over the years. Joanna Dovalis, a Depth Psychologist, also read it more then once. Tim Addey, a scholar at the Prometheus Trust in England went well beyond the task of reading the Plato chapters with his lengthy, generous discourse on the relevant complexities of the philosophy.

Essential thanks to Len Cruz of Chiron Publications who recognized the value in the Platonic Jung and invited me to become part of the Chiron family of authors, as well as polished the manuscript with a great eye for editing detail. Also much appreciation extended to Jennifer Fitzgerald whose editing and organizational efforts in the long approach to the finish line were crucial.

Also, life-long gratitude will always be extended to Dennis Littky, who has been transforming lives for decades by creating schools that truly work. He gave me the opportunity early on in my clinical career to learn how education is essential for healing and growth, and what scholarship, individuality, and creativity can be both personally and professionally. The impact of his work is as vital and alive for me today as it was 35 years ago.

And heartfelt acknowledgement for my husband Morgan McLeod who I feel blessed to have at my side. Words are not adequate to describe my experience but Thank You, Morgan, for your attentive presence as well as everything else. Lets stay together, as Al Green sings to all the lovers who cherish their union.

Table of Contents

Table of Contents

In the products of fantasy the primordial images are made visible and it is here that the concept of the archetype finds its specific application. I do not claim to have been the first to point out this fact. The honor belongs to Plato. (Jung 1968a, 78-79)

Introduction

The aim of this book is to demonstrate that Jung's psychology is rooted in Plato's philosophy, specifically concerning the nature of the cosmos and the individual self. Plato's cosmology consists of levels of being—each representing a different realm while simultaneously remaining a whole, or unity with the others. Jung reiterates these same levels of being in his cosmos where they also represent different realms while remaining a whole or unity. This dynamic of being different, separate, and part, while remaining the same, a unity and whole, I call dual-unity. It is the cornerstone of the cosmology and the nature of the self/Self in both Plato and Jung (self referring to the human individual self and Self to the divine, archetypal Self or One that is the source of the self and cosmos).

The self in both Plato and Jung begins its journey of consciousness in the natural world, lacking awareness of higher realms. Through the process of individuation in Jung and through the application of philosophy in Plato the true individual emerges from this outpost of the natural world, conscious in soul, in what both Plato and Jung called the third, a level of being in-between the higher and lower realms. The individual soul aware in the third remains aware of ego and the world of sense while also able to experience higher dimensions of being, including the source of being in the divine Self or God. The integration and mastery of the lower level of ego and sense in Plato and Jung creates consciousness in soul, which is a consciousness of dual-unity. Awareness of soul's dual-unity changes a person profoundly, giving him or her the capacity to unite with all levels of reality while remaining an individual.

Jung's esotericism is highlighted in this book, which concerns inner transformation. The *Red Book*, a kind of private journal that is also a spectacular illustrated manuscript in the medieval style, is Jung's opus of personal transformation. It illustrates his own consciousness of soul awake in the third located between ego experience shaped and informed by the complexes acquired throughout development (that operate from the unconscious until made partially conscious through individuation), and the higher world of the archetypes and Self. It was Jung's consciousness of soul in the third that enabled his experience of the transcendent Self, which was expressed in the beautifully wrought archetypal images he was able to realize and then concretize for our sensible experience with pencil, ink and paint. The *Red Book* is evidence of Jung's integrated and deeply coherent awareness of all the levels of being expressed through a work of art that is also spiritual science.

Jung kept the *Red Book* hidden even after his death, I suspect because he believed his esotericism would be misunderstood. He did release an excerpt called "Seven Sermons" in his later life, which was not received with enthusiasm. Afterwards Jung did not continue to publish his work from the *Red Book*. It seems he did not want to risk his scientific reputation by revealing the extent of his inner transformative experience. In spite of this caution, Jung was branded a mystic and Analytic Psychology was isolated from contemporary psychoanalytic approaches and neglected by the academy or university setting. This same reticence seems to have prevented him from making his work on the nature of the individual self as soul in the third a central theme in his *Collected Works*.

It is interesting to note that Jung also had a habit of declaring against the metaphysical trends in his work and emphasizing his empiricism. In Civilization in Transition (1970) he states, "It is a common and totally unjustified misunderstanding on the part of scientifically trained people to say I regard the psychic background as something 'metaphysical' while on the other hand the theologians accuse me of 'psychologizing' metaphysics. Both are wide of the mark, I am an empiricist who keeps within the boundaries set for him by the theory of knowledge" (p. 328). Later in the same text he also declares, "I am concerned primarily with the formulation of empirical facts and not with dubious incursions into metaphysics" (p. 410). These comments stand in direct opposition to his most creative contributions. Jung's metaphysical work is the backbone of Analytic Psychology, and it provides every practitioner with the ontological foundation necessary for human healing. Ontology, the branch of metaphysics that deals with the nature of Being, is essential. Without it there is no orientation towards the meaning or nature of Being, therefore, the act of healing has no anchor. I am going to show how Jung's Platonic ontology is the foundation of Analytic Psychology.

I am also going to bring out a perspective on the transcendent function that to my knowledge has not been explored in Jungian studies. Jeffrey Miller's work describes how the transcendent function "has different faces, one moment appearing in one guise, the next in another… it defies clarity."(Miller, 2004, p. 76). Jung seemed to deliberately keep this central concept of his whole theory evolving and open, allowing for new discoveries. It is a testament to Jung's genius that elements of his work are still being uncovered. The aspect of the transcendent function I am concerned with is directly related to his theory of Being (ontology), and the maturation of the human spirit through energetic transformations in the transcendent function and, therefore, the self. Jung referred to this unifying transformation as teleological, meaning there is an inborn, latent pattern of the individual self. This pattern is capable of unifying all levels of Being in the soul. He proposed that each unique Being is actualized slowly through life or, more effectively, through individuation, either in psychotherapy or outside of psychotherapy.

Transformations in healing that lead to awareness of the individuated self or soul beyond the experience of the ego organized by complexes, creates a level of Being Jung refers to as "the whole man" and also as "Christ consciousness." Such transformations represent a new interpretation for the Christian spiritual tradition:

> Instead of using the term God you say "unconscious," instead of Christ "self," instead of incarnation "integration of the unconscious," instead of salvation or redemption "individuation" instead

of crucifixion or sacrifice on the cross "realization of the four functions or of "wholeness" (Jung 1976, p. 736).

The Jung I am bringing out in this work uncovers an evolutionary psychology that propels humankind into a more unified and higher level of Being, while still participating in the ego and physical life. I will argue that Jung uses Plato's cosmology as a base for his own psychology, that he makes a distinction between the individual self and the collective archetype of the Self, and that the Jungian self is Platonic in its nature, dynamic structure, and development. Finally, I will discuss how Jung made various references to the soul having a subtle body of its own, also a Platonic doctrine.

In summary, the first chapters of the book identify the similarities between Plato and Jung's cosmology. The following chapters focus on how both systems include the nature of the individual self as soul in the third with a subtle immaterial body and discussions of transformation through philosophy and individuation. I also include a chapter on praxis for analytically orientated therapists who would like to incorporate the development of the individual self as soul in their own psychotherapeutic work. The first chapter describes my own personal experience of soul in the third, a call that has been answered by my work on this project.

The book mirrors and continues Jung's commitment to Platonic ideas about the nature of the individual soul and the possibility of it existing as a subtle immaterial body. It illuminates the pinnacle of Jung's entire mission, that is: to teach those who are interested that individuation and psychological healing guide a person into awareness of their own soul. Furthermore, that this spiritual individuality is a unique destiny eventually experienced in a simultaneous relationship with ego based sense experience, the archetypes, and the divine archetype of the Self or God.

Chapter One
From Experience to Application

I have followed Jung's dictum "experience without speculation leads nowhere" (Jung 1960, 193), especially in regard to the mystical experiences I have had. From a very young age I was introspective, speculating about the many mysterious and unknown aspects of life. One of these mysteries was an awareness of a part of myself that was an internal witness to my perception, thoughts, feelings, and outer events. This witness occurred simultaneously with my subjective experience but was not the same. I have distinct memories of how this witness related to my direct experience.

For example, I remember one time when my mother was dressing me. I felt uncomfortable as she roughly and quickly squeezed my arms into one sleeve at a time. I lifted my gaze to her face. As I looked into her face this witness made me aware of her mindlessness as she dressed me. I distinctly remember other events like this occurring before I was three years old when autobiographical memory is suggested to begin (Siegel, 1999, p. 35-36).

Another early memory is of crawling as fast as I could behind my sister who was running down a long hallway. I felt painful rug burns on my knees and while this feeling was registering, my witness self reminded me of the helplessness of infancy. Later, while I was learning to walk, I remember standing and throwing myself forward with my arms outstretched in front of me, and then falling. It was this witnessing part of myself that made me aware that repetitively throwing my body forward with my arms outstretched would lead to the desired outcome.

The distinct recall of these early experiences has always led me to speculate upon the nature of reality, my self, and consciousness.

Eventually in high school I began to examine the nature of Being and become interested in consciousness. Although I went to college, secured a Bachelors in Education, and began teaching, consciousness was what I wanted to study. Thus, I went on to earn a Masters in Counseling and a Doctorate in Clinical Psychology. As of the present moment I have been in clinical practice for thirty-five years and still remain inspired.

During my freshman year in college I devoted myself to focusing on dreams and the dreamy yet wakeful state, known as the hypnogogic state, that occurs before sleep. When I was eighteen and in my second semester I had my first experience of consciousness in the subtle soul-body during one of these hypnogogic states. The experience was (and is) one of being out of the physical body in another more subtle body of immaterial matter. In these states I was still aware of my separate physical body and world. After my brief voyage at eighteen, I wrote in my journal the phrase "inward certitude" to describe and express my knowledge that this anomalous event was somehow a life call.

This experience frightened me and struck me in several other ways. I felt a new degree of mental clarity and I felt more alive. All my senses seemed heightened and my mind seemed sharper. I felt a lifting of restriction or liberation from my rational, sense-based mind along with a new awareness of my intuitive Being. These impressions ignited a deep need to learn as much as possible about subtle body phenomenon. Immediately after my "call" in 1977, I began decades of study in religion, philosophy, psychology, history, science, and other fields in order to develop knowledge about this experience. I also embarked on a steady spiritual practice along with exploring the dynamic unconscious in psychotherapy, all of which helped me understand myself.

My very first experience of consciousness in my subtle soul-body began with a roaring in my ears, utter paralysis of motion, and vibrations sweeping throughout my body. Suddenly I felt a magnetic force from my solar plexus or heart area. I catapulted out of my body. I remained separated from and above my physical body for what must have been only seconds. I knew I had left my body and felt myself "out." Just as suddenly I returned "inside" the flesh. I lay there fearfully, wondering if I had some kind of heart attack or stroke.

The next day I visited my psychology professor to talk with her about it and she gave me several books, including Bob Monroe's *Journeys Out of Body* (1971). After my undergraduate studies and also equipped with a Master's degree in Counseling I went to the Monroe Institute where Bob Monroe's patented technology was applied to willing investigators. This technology synchronized the two hemispheres of the brain. In a two-week long seminar I experienced several levels of altered states. After the seminar experience I moved to Virginia and worked in the Institute lab for a summer. The following year when I got my first psychotherapy job at a public mental health clinic in Virginia, I joined the Institute's professional research organization. At that time in the early eighties there was an active and international membership pursuing knowledge of altered states both in the laboratory and clinical setting. As time passed, I did not keep up with the Institute, nor was I impressed with Monroe's later books. The original mission seemed to have shifted over the years from an academic bent to a New Age and commercial focus.

I think of my subtle body experiences as a kind of grace because I don't think I create it on my own, rather I dispose myself as best I can and wait. I remain a beginner, in both understanding and skills, even after decades of inquiry.

The first ten years of my experience were marked by a difficult entry into this subtle, soul-body consciousness, heralded by a roaring in my ears and magnetic rhythmic forces impacting my body, especially around my heart. The magnetic rhythmic force seemed like powerful waves that had a kind of substance or weight. About every two years, I would experience these vibratory phenomena when my consciousness was between waking and sleeping. A primary aspect of the experience continued to be overwhelming fear, which hindered my capacity to get much further than leaving my physical body. I worked hard these years at controlling the irrational leap into fear hoping I could handle "the unknown," successfully. I felt despair when, as always, I would succumb to instinctual energies. I didn't want to lose control of my body or my life in a "normal" world.

For three years after graduating college, I lived in a small, isolated cabin on a mountain in New Hampshire, Pudding Hill, where I had no running water or electricity and built an attached greenhouse to grow vegetables. In those three years I understood how little it takes to live well, and what deep simplicity means on a practical level. The discipline of "chop wood, carry water," especially through the long snowy northern winters, laid the foundation for my spiritual, philosophical, ecological, and political life. Living on Pudding Hill taught me many things, especially how to relate to our consumer driven world. Most importantly, it reinforced and developed my tendency towards inwardness, solitude and quiet, even though I remained busy teaching movement dance, going to graduate school, and commuting to Massachusetts for a full time internship.

When I finished graduate school I moved from New England to Virginia and began working as a therapist at a mental health clinic. I also entered my own psychotherapy. My deeper passion was my study and practice of Gurdjieff's Fourth Way, an esoteric philosophy recorded by Dr. Maurice Nicoll in a five-volume work called the "Psychological Commentaries" (1957, 1960).

The Fourth Way

The Fourth Way is a method of developing consciousness that was originally introduced to the world by G.I. Gurdjieff (1870-1949). An esoteric philosopher, Gurdjieff developed the Fourth Way for people who lived everyday lives; thus, it is called the way of the householder. The Fourth Way develops the self using normal experience as the material to transform consciousness—this is in contrast to the Way of the Yogi, Monk, or Fakir that are singular paths of the heart, mind, or body respectively. Maurice Nicoll, a psychiatrist, was a pupil of Gurdjieff's and was also a student of Jung's. In the chapter on praxis I integrate some of the wealth of wisdom found in the Fourth Way into the practice of psychotherapy.

The Psychological Commentaries on the Teaching of Gurdjieff and Ouspensky include detailed instructions of working with the attention. Along with practicing with my attention during my waking hours I used the Fourth Way as a method of training my attention while doing psychotherapy. Referred to as "work on the self," these practices attempt to transform the multiple awareness of ego into a single consciousness of empty, observing witness. The witness is able to hold the opposites together; for example, it is both a forgetting of self and remembering of self. I noticed that through my practice of the Fourth Way method my witness self came closer and it was more powerful. This knowing witness or presence was expressed during the therapeutic hour in a heightened intersubjective field, a connection between the patient and myself that was also a unitive state. I borrow the term "unitive" from the Christian mystic tradition. It describes an experience of oneself and another as both one and two, separate and unified at the same time. This term "unitive" is found in the writings of two of my favorite teachers, the Spanish mystic St. Theresa of Avila (Collected Works, 1946) and the more modern British woman who also walked the mystic path, Evelyn Underhill (Mysticism, 1960).

The unitive state is akin to a mystical state, where two people comprise one unified experience at the same time as remaining separate. Attempting to develop the capacity to experience the dual-unity at the root of mystical experience is a goal of working on the self in the Fourth Way. Nicoll (1957a, 935) describes this purpose in the *The Psychological Commentaries on the Teaching of Gurdjieff and Ouspensky* as "sacrificing personality for essence," which means emptying the small self or ego in order to experience and develop spiritual awareness in soul. The Fourth Way is a complex method that is well described in the *The Psychological Commentaries on the Teaching of Gurdjieff and Ouspensky*. According to the Fourth Way, sacrificing the ego or personality for essence involves energetic transformations that develop consciousness of essence or soul, as well as the subtle body of soul.

Over the years I have continuously pursued clinical training, for example in family therapy, child development, play therapy, hospice training, grief and loss, and especially contemporary psychoanalytic methods and related research on affect regulation and attachment. In my early thirties I returned with more concentration to Jungian psychology—the field that initially attracted me to the profession.

Despite considerable training in psychotherapy, my practice of esoteric philosophy has given me more actual lift into the mysteries of human being. In my supervision work I began to teach my own method of psychotherapy combining both clinical psychology and Gurdjieff's esoteric work on the self.

Subtle Soul-Body Awareness

After more than a decade of episodic experience of subtle body, at twenty-nine years of age I finally reached a new threshold during the conscious shift out of the physical body. Constant work with my attention, my personal spiritual practice, disciplined study, work in depth psychotherapy, and dietary restrictions reduced the jarring, noisy transitions of my earlier experience.

With this new transition out of body I had the familiar feeling of being paralyzed in the sweeping vibrations but now it was a gentle holding rather than a grip on my physical body. The noise in my ears became a low, even hum. The wave-force movement was now a slight pressure on my solar plexus that resulted in an immediate arching out of the physical body. For many years I struggled with lengthy, loud, and disorganizing forces, but now I moved into the subtle body quickly and smoothly.

Along with the easy and quick exit my immediate instinctual terror was gone. My fear was no longer a reaction; it became a more deliberate holding of myself: my body still and my mind empty. On this occasion I floated up from my physical body like a buoy bobbing up and down and slowly looked back at the bed where I saw my own form as well as my husband's under the covers. I moved with no thought towards the shadowy light coming into the room from the heating vent in the wall. This small vent conveyed heat from the living room and it reflected a dim light from the kitchen night-light.

Internally still and quiet, I floated toward the dim light with my knees bent and my arms loose. I slowly went into the space right in front of this vent, with a linen chest on the left, the wall on the right, and books above me. I had curled up in order to fit into what was a smallish "space." I remained there momentarily looking around. As I thought about not knowing what was happening, I felt a rush of insecurity and returned to my physical body so instantaneously I was not able to hold in my mind the travel I obviously made in order to reoccupy my body.

Throughout my thirties I usually remained within sight of my bed after exiting the physical body. Leaving grew easier with very even sensations and very slight noise.

Re-entry into the physical body from the subtle soul body ranged from instant awakening to chaotic falling that left me disoriented without direction. In this latter instance I was confused about where I was even after opening my physical eyes.

I also have experiences of seeing into the subtle soul world without leaving my physical body. When in college I began seeing colorful energy around people, usually around the head. I learned that these colors are referred to as the aura and realized that if I concentrated sufficiently I could bring these colors alive at will. Sometimes I can see auras without effort.

In my twenties I had an experience of seeing into the subtle world that was associated with covetous desire, the shadow existing in opposition to my conscious efforts to relinquish material greed. In bed late at night I thought about and at the same time visualized a scarf that belonged to someone I knew, but had been left behind in a lost-and-found box at a music club I used to frequent. I had picked it up in order to return it to its owner. I sat up feeling that I wanted this scarf for myself, wondering how I could keep it. Immediately I saw and felt a black life form land on my left shoulder. It had a head and body and very short limbs and was about the length of my forearm. Like an impish animal with a certain human quality, I could feel its cunning and intention. It actually dug its claws into my shoulder.[1]

I felt its power. A negative, suppressing, and possessive quality attached itself to me. This was a sensation that did not hurt my physical body but made me afraid. The entity grabbed onto me in a sort of gleeful way. I immediately began to pray and within seconds I felt like this entity

---

[1] See E. Swedenborg, (1688-1772), Spiritual Experiences 1745-1765, Vol. I, (trans.). D. Odhner, Bryn Athyn, Penn: Church of the New Jerusalem for further discussion of thought forms as entities. A world-renowned scientist and inventor identified as a genius along with Goethe and John Stuart Mill by a study at Stanford University, Swedenborg became clairvoyant in later life. He is considered to have been a significant influence in several areas of Western culture.

(if that was what it was) was forced, reluctantly, to relinquish its hold upon me. This was the first experience I had of the protective power of prayer. The next day I got up and returned the scarf. This experience seems to suggest , like Swedenborg has reported (see footnote), that there are life forms present within thought and furthermore that they inform attitude, intention, and act with power and substance to create good and evil. A moral life is developed through conscious control of thought, intention and act and is shaped by free will.

When I am awake in this other world, conscious of being aware in my subtle body, I focus on my perception and inner senses. I practice maintaining my focus and concentration so I can remember everything about the experience. I deliberately concentrate on my self as rarified substance and on my physical self, which is visible through my eyes and knowable through an energetic or instinctual affinity that seems to be some kind of sense. I focus on my surroundings, the things in the "space," and any other distinct features such as the quality of the light. I do not will myself to other locations beyond the vicinity of my physical body because I am still fearful, and recognize my limits mastering this unknown world. In my more radical experiences, I seem to be taken there regardless of my will. Although I feel I have "come a long way" in this state of being conscious in my subtle soul-body, I am undeveloped. I believe that becoming more developed in subtle soul-body consciousness is part of a universal human evolution.

Dream Work

In dream work there is awareness of a different subject/object boundary than in the subtle world. Subject/object boundary refers to the experience one has of the self in relation to an "other," an object that is distinct yet connected to the self in the inner world and outer. This "object" in relation to the self usually consists of things, spaces and persons, but can also include realms. Jung helps us conceptualize this internal self/object boundary when he distinguishes between the subjective or personal unconscious, which is the reservoir of personal experience collected throughout life and the objective unconscious. The objective unconscious is a realm that is different from the images in the personal unconscious that are also objects. The collective unconscious is objective, separate from one's inner experience. It is a higher, spiritual, archetypal "other" sourced outside the personal or subjective unconscious. It is an objective realm that is phenomenologically real yet also experienced subjectively.

Application in Practice

Normal dreams and reveries leave the sense of a dream image that is mostly organized from the subjective or personal unconscious, although it has archetypal content within it. In these states dreaming originates from the personal self. Sometimes a numinous dream occurs that is lucid movement into the objective unconscious. Sometimes numinous dreams can predict the future. Jung referred to this kind of dream as a "big dream." He had a famous dream of this type predicting the world war. Unlike an ordinary dream, subtle soul-body consciousness is an experience of crossing a boundary where one is aware that the subjective sense of self occurs within the larger objective realm. While dreams venture over the threshold of consciousness into a deeper subjectivity, subtle soul-body consciousness is a movement through this deeper subjectivity into a larger objective reality. It is a threshold to extra-mundane worlds.

In view of subtle soul-body being a link between the subjective and objective realms and a mysterious threshold into other worlds, it seems important to realize that the condition of one's Being will in some way determine the kind of experience one has (just like the condition of one's Being influences awareness of the outside, physical world). Integration of traumatic unconscious contents and the ability to adequately manage one's own conscious inner landscape seem a prerequisite for avoiding the phenomenology of unrealized shadow elements in the subtle soul realm. Like seems to attract like in the subtle soul world as in the physical world, but with much more sensitivity and greater magnetic power. Whatever thought a person harbors could be an encounter with a definite and distinct energetic force. It could be that our dense physicality is actually a protection from subtle realities we should remain unaware of until we are more developed. In view of this, I guard against disorganized and uncontrolled episodes in the subtle soul world by steady and habitual efforts to work on myself. I will always continue working toward that esoteric balance that expresses itself in a level of control that is a perfect spontaneity.

Plato's philosophy centered on virtue, Esoteric Christianity's emphasis on sacrifice and purification, and occult practices insisting on discipline and control all touch the same essential chords in authentic, psycho-spiritual advancement. Safe and conscious experience of awareness in subtle soul-body seems to imply adequate healing of one's personal psychology and skillful control of impulse, feeling, and thought, as well as bodily discipline. Control of oneself through the threshold brings one into a mode that is also life in another dimension, albeit a dimension that seems to be in very close proximity to the physical.

Subtle soul-body experience seems to reveal or manifest the things one loves, which create the condition of one's Being. What one loves is not content of mind but substrate of mind. The content of one's thoughts (thinking in this context includes affect) forms and changes one's Being. These two, thinking and Being, are inextricably linked and shape subtle soul-body experience. If one's mind is identified mostly with ego-laden values, one's Being will mirror or reflect these loves. Or, if a person is emotionally ill and preoccupied with negative states, the subtle soul realm, if it opens to this person, may tend towards lack of light, chaos, and negativity. For example, I saw a patient who was very sensitive and gifted but very ill, who reported several terrifying out of body experiences of the subtle soul world, and the forces within it.

Subtle soul experience brought on by fragmentation and dissociation seems to present an out-of-control chaos, whereas a more integrated and coherent sense of self seems to present benign and positive realms. Those who have developed a steady practice of witness presence may have a subtle soul experience that I refer to as the light of Christ. Christ, for me, is a state of being in unity with the Divine. Jesus is an individual soul who has achieved this Christ consciousness and therefore is a God-man and wisdom teacher who is present as a guide to those who are interested in finding the divine ground in the depths of their own being.

My experience of this light within is one of a unified level of Being as well as a "who," or a presence. When I have had brief experiences of this subtle soul state I feel aware of a sweetness, joy, bliss, peace, freedom, and love, and none of these words completely explain it. Difficult or even impossible to explain (like any ethereal or transcendent experience), I feel a light that is at the same time an interior substance. Finding this interior experience is directly related to eliminating internal activity and achieving a necessary degree of presence to the empty self or ego. An opening to mystical states, empty self is not losing or annihilating the self. Rather, it is a purifying of self. A purifying of consciousness involves a letting go of everything but an awareness of divine presence. This awareness is a personal experience of open presence or waiting.

When considering the many kinds of subtle soul-body experience I have had, it seems that the subtle soul-body realm may be as St. Theresa in her book *The Interior Castle* refers to as consisting of "many mansions," or dimensions of experience. When I have been conscious of awareness in the subtle soul-body, the same spaces where I live physically are very obviously represented in a different dimension. Seeing my physical form lying prone on the bed suggests that the subtle soul realm and the physical realm are two different yet connected, spatially extended places. I have been vast distances away from my body and home, yet able to reflect on how I am somewhere that is a "place" not hemmed in by space or time. Through these experiences, I am aware that our apprehension of our universe and ourselves is presently very limited, and the next and last unexplored frontier is the interior world.

Subtle soul-body awareness has taught me that the emotional, cognitive, and spiritual worlds are intertwined. This intertwined relationship invokes ontology, or questions/theories about the nature of Being for any psychotherapist, whether or not he/she is conscious of it. My ontological stance has developed out of my experiences of subtle soul-body consciousness. I know through experience that awareness in subtle soul-body has a critical place in physical, cognitive, emotional, and spiritual life. It is my innermost voice, the organ of intuition, and a vehicle for subtle perceptions and knowing beyond the brain and five senses of the physical body. It creates a level of physical sensitivity that translates into heightened body awareness. It is the source of emotion, and the agent of healing. Not least, it is a doorway into another dimension of self and of reality.

Jung's Psychology

These considerations make way for important shifts in our traditional understanding of analytic psychology. Jung's philosophical and metaphysical work about the individual soul and his comments about the existence of a subtle soul-body go beyond the healing of the dynamic complex and/or experience of numinosity in the archetype of the Self or God Image. Clarifying the theoretical dimension of individual self as soul addresses the development of attributes of consciousness that result from spiritual awareness. Jung's psychology is known for the unique experience of spirit in the numinosity of the archetype, and especially of the archetype of the Self. Jung's work on the individual soul in relation with the archetype of the Self brings archetypal, spiritual qualities into the possession of individual character as specific virtues. Thus the psyche expands from healing opposites in the ego complexes on the personal level and the experience of the archetype of the Self, to the permanent, transcendent experience of soul and its attributes on the individual level.

Jung is the first theoretical psychologist to attempt to describe the energetic nature of healing and its operations and transformations within the human being. I will describe these actions when I discuss the transcendent function later on. Jung's association with Wolfgang Pauli (one of the founders of quantum physics) perhaps helped in synthesizing his earlier work on the energetic aspect of the transcendent function into his conclusions on the existence of an energetic, psychoid realm, which I will also discuss later on. In *Mysterium Coniunctionis* (1970), Jung discusses the parallels between the quantum and psychological worlds:

> Microphysics is feeling its way into the unknown side of matter, just as complex psychology is pushing forward into the unknown side of the psyche . . . the common background of microphysics and depth-psychology is as much physical as psychic and therefore neither, but rather a third thing. (p. 538)
>
> A synthesis of the conscious with the unconscious … is theoretically inconceivable, since a known quantity is combined with an unknown one; but in practice as many far-reaching changes of consciousness result from it, as atomic physics has produced in classical physics. (p. 538)

Jung is describing that as our awareness of the physical universe moves into the quantum level and our awareness of the conscious mind moves into the unconscious, we discover a background, linking element, which is a third thing. The third thing is both physical and psychic, and something else that transcends both. The integration of these two dimensions and subsequent awareness of the third creates radical shifts in consciousness, like the transformations that occurred when the discoveries of the quantum world displaced classical physics.

In human consciousness, awareness of the common ground or third emerges when one intentionally links conscious experience to unconscious experience. In the earlier quotes Jung equates the unconscious with the quantum and the conscious with the classical world of matter. Jung was aware within his own soul and thus traveled between these worlds. His genius portrayed these experiences, elevating human understanding from the concrete into the symbolic image and beyond into the transcendent and invisible worlds.

In my experience, the transcendent, invisible, subtle soul world has substance and form like the physical, but of a more rarified nature. Subtle soul substance seems to hold form exactly like grosser matter, yet moves instantaneously with thought and desire unless these are not present—then there is stillness or floating. The subtle soul world seems spatially extended and substantial, distinct from the physical as well as connected. It may be that the subtle soul world and the physical realms are distinct yet connected because of the relativity of vibratory motion between the energy of the physical body and the energy of the more rarified subtle body.

Energy is always moving, and it may be that achieving a constant and steady velocity of motion in the different energy bodies creates consciousness of the link between the realms or bodies. Achieving this link creates the experience of connection where there is a seemingly motionless harmony of both worlds. I believe it was the uneven motion of my energy bodies that caused the jarring, frightening, and static-like vibrations I experienced for years. Reaching a steadiness of motion between bodies happened through developing my consciousness, which was then liberated in the more rarified body and able to bridge a gap in our usual perceptions. This bridge (the soul) appears to extend and unify consciousness of life within the individual. When one experiences these processes, one knows intuitively that there is something happening in the space/time/motion continuum.

The science of special relativity has revealed the subjective nature of space/time/motion dynamics, something that usually goes unnoticed due to minute differences in individual perception. One must move at speeds close to the speed of light to realize these differences. If String Theory (a recent explanatory model within subatomic particles physics) is substantiated, our understanding of reality will be re-organized into a many dimensional model comprised of minute units of vibrating energy/matter. As energy becomes more rarified and less dense, it quickens its rate of motion towards pure light and has a higher vibration and frequency, all of which translate into a higher con-sciousness. The subtlest, most developed soul-body is that of pure light. To whatever degree possible, the "man of light" (Corbin, 1994) becomes consciously embodied within physical matter through the unifying of the gross body with the subtle soul-body, signifying a step toward wholeness. Like any developmental process, awareness in the subtle soul-body must grow, perhaps from a state of dim and dense awareness to greater degrees of rare and increasingly refined light energy. The awareness of soul consciousness exists in many different degrees according to an individual's capacity.

Unlike other approaches that emphasize ego function, Analytic Psychology is distinct in recognizing the unifying and elevating function of the archetypes and the archetype of the Self, beyond adequate ego functioning. Through integration and transcendence of opposites and awareness of the archetype and the archetype of the Self knowledge and experience of spiritual reality can be realized. Today it is important for all of us, but especially the psychological community, to recognize another stage of growth between the healing of the complex and the ultimate flashpoint of numinous experience of the archetype of the Self. This stage is the development of the individual self in soul, and perhaps even an awareness of its subtle body. This development must be individual, and is not the transcendent archetype, the archetype of the Self, or the ego and its complexes. The degree of awareness of soul a person has realized reflects the level at which a person has individuated, or become a true individual, beyond ego consciousness.

Consciousness of the true individual has characteristics that differentiate it from the finite ego. The true individual is no longer driven by the collective experience and also expresses an elevated and unified state of Being with qualities that have historically been recognized as spiritually derived. Such spiritual values are received through transcendent resources, when the opposites in the psyche have been adequately united. Each individual who has reached some degree of this form of consciousness becomes a force in the healing of themselves, of persons in relationship to them, of our nation, and our suffering earth and her creatures. All these effects are achieved through awareness of soul, of a unified and elevated consciousness and its natural radiation outward into others and the world.

In our current thinking and habit of practicing analytic psycho-therapy, healing occurs in the emotional, cognitive, and physical domains, and spiritually through the influence of the archetype. Jung's work on soul as the nature of the individual self adds significantly to the emotional and spiritual healing that occurs in therapy, as well as introduces an energetic dimension of healing that is essential for the rest. We will see how energetic transformations promote human development, when therapist and patient knit together the various splits that exist in the psyche due to oppositions in the complexes, especially those acquired through injury and defense. These splits are in affectively sequestered experiences in the inner world where feelings become walled off and isolated from the sense of self, each other, and other functions of the personality, like the intellect or the physical body. The fragmentation and isolation in the human psyche due to wounds received to the growing self, and the natural oppositions in the complexes, are unfortunately mirrored in our global culture. As significant numbers of people heal themselves, the balance and unity achieved by the individual will be reflected in the balance and unity of the world.

Depth psychology can influence change towards a more balanced global culture by following Jung into his hidden ontological depth about the nature of the individual self as soul. As I mentioned earlier, Jung believed energetic transformations in the human psyche could be aligned with what we have discovered in physics. Such energetic transformations can also be aligned today with the contemporary paradigm of Wholeness Science in biology. The epistemology in Wholeness Science is especially relevant to an Analytic Psychology that includes the individual self as soul, which is an invisible, energetic and self-organizing force emerging into consciousness.

Wholeness Science begins with unity rather than separation, is participatory, includes our inner experiences, and involves understanding as well as prediction and control. Three important variables characterize this science and reveal the subtle, invisible relationships hidden in our tangible world. The first variable is the recognition that wholes are *more* than the sum of their parts. This idea moves us beyond the schema that organisms and life forms can be fully known and measured by taking them apart. The second variable considers *emergent qualities* that cannot be reduced even in principle to the physical sciences. Thirdly, and most radical, this new holistic science has the insight that *consciousness* appears or seems to be present as a substrate of physical reality (Harman, Sahtouris 1996, x).

To be conscious is "to be subjectively known or felt" and consciousness is defined as "awareness" (Webster, 1995). That there appears to be a fundamental, self-organizing force, subjectively aware, knowing and feeling its self in all living systems remains unexplainable by empirical science or current physical principles (Harman, Sahtouris 1996, x). This unexplainable self-organizing force shows up as teleological, i.e., purposely informing development in organisms that cannot be separated from their environment. Life appears and persists in this model as a single ecology. The creation of form in this web (and I include the human form here) is seen to be a dynamic process in which genes play a distinctive but limited role. New research in epigenetic's may be pointing this way. Emergent processes are considered to be the central quality of creation and evolution, and these processes have yet to be understood.

These ideas and model of knowledge can be applied to depth psychology and Jung himself wrote about such phenomena. The new models "single ecology" where all life is linked mirrors Jung's description of the connection between the unified and transcendent archetype and its psychic image experienced in the human personality, which Jung called the "psychic fact" (1969, 328, 353). From the perspective of this paradigm, Jung's idea of the complex connected to the archetypal, collective, unconscious can be expanded to include the existence of an invisible, creatively emergent, and participatory self-organizing process, which is the individual consciousness or soul. Furthermore, that soul exists whether or not a person is conscious of it and that becoming conscious of it is a healing and evolutionary step. It seems that the individual consciousness or soul has a subtle energetic matter, and that it is located in a third ontological realm bridging the archetypal world (with the Self at its center), and the ego and its complexes. As such, the soul orchestrates life in the physical body and is a primary force in human development and growth. Jung remarks that "*consciousness is a precondition of being,*" (1970, 271) and postulates that consciousness is an archetypal, cosmic, metaphysical principle that supports, conditions, and promotes our everyday experience and our personal growth. Deferring to his teachers, Jung declares that Analytic Psychology is spiritually based:

A modern scientific psychology which starts from the spirit . . . [and is] based on the postulate of an autonomous, spiritual

principle…[supposes] that the psyche arises from a spiritual
principle . . . We must turn back to the teachings of our forefathers
for it was they who made such assumptions. (Jung 1969c, 344-345).

Based on the strong parallels that exist between Jung and Plato, it is
likely that Jung had Plato in mind when referring to "our forefathers."
What follows is an exploration of the Platonic roots of Jung's Analytic
Psychology, especially concerning the nature of the self.

Chapter 2
The Cosmology

"Quantum Physics thus reveals a basic oneness of the Universe."
Edwin Schrodinger

The Platonic opus is very complex, so much so that scholars still continue to find material to debate after centuries and even millennia. I find Jung's *Collected Works* similar in their complexity. Both men present varying points of view depending on where they were in their own development over a lifetime of work, and sometimes these views conflict. There is a fundamental resemblance in the way Plato and Jung fashion the universe, both the inner and outer cosmology of human experience. I will follow a thread of Plato that is embedded in a whole fabric, the totality of which is beyond my capacity or intent to unravel. I do not intend to make an exhaustive analytic study of the differences and the similarities between Plato and Jung. Rather, my intention is to show practicing psychologists as well as interested nonprofessionals how Jung used Plato's work to both define his own cosmology and the development of the soul as an individual self.

In Plato the structure of the universe is the One, the intelligible realm and Form, and the sensible/physical world. The whole of this macro-cosmos is mirrored internally in the human micro-cosmos. Each level of this structure remains separate but also exists as a unity, and a person can become aware of the whole and part simultaneously. With Jung this structure is repeated in the macro-cosmos of Self, the archetypal realm and archetype and the sense based or sensible experience of the ego and the various personal complexes acquired in relation to the physical world. Like in Plato's cosmology, the whole is mirrored internally in the micro-cosmos of the human psyche. Also in Jung the totality or the unity exists simultaneously with each different and distinct level, and every individual can potentially experience the whole and part together.

In both systems the nature of the true individual is soul coming to awareness at the cosmic mid-point or third, able to realize the whole as a "center existing within, yet paradoxically at the same time, without" (Jung 1969a, 169). Linking the inner with the outer, the higher with the lower, developing consciousness in soul was the central mission for both Plato and Jung.

Some Considerations on the Platonic One

Over time, translations of Plato's cosmology have changed.[1] Ancient translations included the One as an ontological category, the beginning, unity and source of all Being. In the twentieth century an important shift occurred in which Plato's cosmology was reduced to the intellect and sensible/sensory realms, leaving out the One.[2] This debate is centered on the nature of the One in the dialogue *Parmenides*, as well as other comments about the Good (another name for the One) being a Form in the intellect that is separated from other Forms— a kind of first principle that is not a primary ontological category.

---

[1] Tim Addey of the Prometheus Trust where Thomas Taylor's translations of Greek philosophy are published, has consulted at length on these points. He clarifies the complexity of the ancient translations as compared to the modern. The ancients had access to the original oral traditions, which were intended to instill wisdom in the disciple. Unfortunately, this intention is not meaningful in today's scholarship.

[2] Verity Harte, Ph.D. of Yale University, commenting from the more modern perspective, kindly shared with me her own understanding of current translations. She strongly emphasized the controversial nature of the One in current debates.

When I refer to the "One" in this discussion I will be referring to the traditional translations rather than the contemporary debates. Tim Addey of the Prometheus Trust that publishes Thomas Taylor's work, pointed out to me that there is a distinction in Taylor's translation about the nature of the One. The next few paragraphs are a summary statement of what I have learned from this scholar about the Nature of the One in Taylor. The particular distinction is between the super-essential One, the beginning that exists beyond all Being, and the One-Being, which comes after the superessential. The superessential One is non-being, a simple, perfect unity. The super-essential One "exhibits" because it is prior to creation. In order to create there must be other conditions present.

In Taylor, the super-essential One "exhibits" the One-Being, and the One-Being then exhibits the intellect. The intellect, in turn, is the level of reality that first creates; it creates the soul and the sensible world. The intellect can create because the One-Being from which it emerges includes principles called the bound and the infinite. These two principles are conditions that allow Being to appear in the One-being and then in intellect and soul. Although Plato refers to the natural world as non-being, he contradicts himself by saying that Being exists in the sensible world in the present moment, while the future and past are becoming and therefore non-being. Since the soul and sensible world are "created" rather than exhibited, their Being and substance are different from the earlier levels. All the levels always remain a unity through the principle of the infinite and at the same time are different from one another (differentiated) since they are defined by the principle of the bound. This is hard to grasp. It seems the principle of the bound can be equated with the boundaries inherent in difference and the principle of infinity with identity, sameness and unity in the One.

These considerations help us understand the particulars of creation in Plato's cosmology, especially the relationship of the bound and infinite to the ideas of the same and different and the one and the many, themes that are crucial to understand how the universe occurs and exists as a whole and also as parts. These crucial themes come together into a dynamic that I call dual-unity; this is the heart of Plato and Jung's cosmology. Dual-unity is the cornerstone and central dynamic that allows for hierarchical realities to participate in other levels while remaining different, in both the cosmic and human spheres. Unity allows for the connections between levels, differentiation the separations.

The One at the center of the universe is the beginning and source of Plato's cosmology. Although it is impossible to know with certainty, after reading the *Dialogues* and the *Collected Works* I have concluded that Jung used the traditional translation of the One as a separate ontological category yet without Taylor's distinction of the super-essential One. Jung's concept of the Self resembles the nature of the One (excepting Thomas Taylor's more esoteric rendition) as a simple, transcendent unity that is the source of all Being and life.

In order to illustrate how the One appears in subsequent levels of Being or creation and clarify in general the Platonic doctrine of hypostasis (a level of Being participating in and existing as the center of the next level), Tim Addey, in a personal communication, uses the metaphor of a parent's DNA "participating in" the creation of his or her child. He explained to me that the DNA of the parent creates the child in a fundamental way yet the child also exists on its own. Likewise, each level of reality in Plato "participates" in other levels that are exhibited or created, while existing on its own. The lower level remains passive to the higher held within it, because of the higher level's formative power. Similarly, a child must remain passive (receptive) to his or her parents' DNA, because of its formative power.

It is important to realize that the One (and all the other levels that descend) do not exist in a relation of strict duality because they do not exist totally separate from one another in a state of opposition nor complement. Each exists in connection as well as separation, in unity as well as differentiation; it is the same but different, is bound yet infinite. A person can understand that this arrangement of a higher level forming and participating in the next level begins with the One. It continues through the intellect-also called the intelligible sphere-and the sensible man. The whole always resides in the part.

These dynamics hold true for Jung also, that is the Self "participates in" each archetype, helping to form it, and the archetypal world is within each ego-complex "participating in" or helping to form it. The whole composite is therefore within each complex experienced and expressed in the ego. Soul in both Plato's philosophy and Jung's psychology exists and is created in the transcendent realm, i.e., the intelligible and archetypal world, in-between the higher One or Self and lower sense and ego worlds. Soul descends into the physical world of sense and ego in order to consciously ascend back to its source and in doing so the soul spans the whole cosmology.

In Plato, each level of reality hidden within the other can potentially be known through relationship. While Being is radiated with the One into the intelligible sphere and cascades downward, it becomes conscious in relationship because Being and creation are reflective. In the process, one level looking at the other level can know it and become self aware; this reflective act is the birth of being as knowledge. As knowing and being come together in this act of consciousness, the dynamic of dual-unity within the cosmos becomes conscious. It is this paradoxical condition that defines a two that is also a one, a state of differentiation in unity. Being in soul can reflect on the One above and the world of ego or sense below and experience or know it. Thus the ego or sense based man can reflect the soul above and experience and know the transcendent realm, which includes the One since it is at the center of that same transcendent realm.

The One corresponds to and resembles Jung's archetype of the Self. These two principalities share important attributes and I will explore their similarities next.

The Self and the One

The Divine Center

Jung's archetype of the Self (also referred to as Self) parallels Plato's One in its unity and transcendent divinity. Equally as important, it resembles the One in its nature as the source and totality of all being. As the source of all being the One and Self both appear at the center of subsequent hierarchies of Being. The Self is in the center of every archetype like the One appears at the center of every Form. In turn, the Form and archetype are behind or in the center of every Platonic Form copy in the sensible world and Jungian image in the ego complex, defining phenomenological reality in the physical sphere. Like Plato's One, the archetype of the Self is collective (collective meaning a unity common to every person) and can be known and experienced individually.

According to Jung the conscious integration of the complexes into the ego brings about awareness of the archetypal image and psychoid archetype and therefore the Self at the center of the archetype. In Plato, conscious mastery of the sense based or sensible aspect of the self brings in a subsequent awareness of the intelligible realm and Form and therefore the One at the center of the Form. Soul, the human essence in both systems, is a transcendent level of being that descends into the physical sphere and is the agent of awareness.

Plato identifies the One with a transcendent light that is manifest in all the realms, is unchanging and invisible to the physical eye. The physical light of the sun is the last manifestation of the light of the One. The light that is the One, Plato also refers to as the Good: "The idea of the good ... that this is indeed the cause for all things, of all that is right and beautiful, giving birth in the visible world to light, and the author of light and itself in the intelligible world..." (Plato, 1961, *Republic VII*, 749-750). This light that is the One is also the center and circumference of a circle. In the Timaeus Plato describes how the artificer or creator made the world in the form of a globe, round as a lathe, having its extremes in every direction equidistant from the center, the most perfect and the most like itself of all figures…the movement suited to his spherical form was assigned … he was made to move in the same manner and on the same spot, within his own limits revolving in a circle. (p. 1164)

Plato (1961, 1165) also says a bit further down in the dialogue that the creator "made the universe a circle moving in a circle." This circle moves continually back into the One.

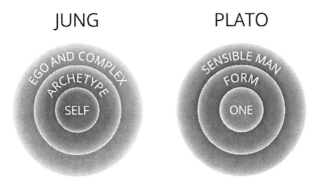

Plato's One is the divine totality of all being. It is infinite and un-created while appearing in lower hierarchies of being. Jung's Self shares these attributes, being the divine totality of all being, infinite and un-created while descending into more limited conditions. These limits can be transcended through individuation but are always a part of the whole, so one never extinguishes them. An individual can experience the Self emotionally and spiritually but the human being is by nature something else, so while unified with the center, he or she remains separate from and in relationship to the infinite divine.

Jung's Self echoes the characteristics of Plato's One in that it is di-vine, a light, and the totality that is a circle, center, and circumference. In the *Collected Works* Jung (1969c, 55) identifies the Self or God as "the essence of spiritual light" and as numinous, which means divine, holy, and spiritual. Jung says that God and the Self "rest on an identical numinous factor which is a condition of reality" (1970b, 546). In *The Archetypes and the Collective Unconscious* Jung describes the circularity of the cosmos by saying that Self and God are an infinite circle and sphere (1968a, 325). Jung uses the image of the mandala (a round Form) to express the Self as circle, center, and circumference. It is the symbol of the Self or the totality of Being, which according to Jung has a "circular motion . . . which everywhere returns into itself" (Jung 1971, 326). The Self and the One descend as a circle and center into the archetype and Form, which then descends as a center and circle into the ego's complexes and sensible world. I have included a diagram of this image on the previous page. Consciousness in the world of ego and sense circles around the whole, potentially reaching the center through philosophy or individuation.

The soul is also part of this cosmic circle. Jung (1969a) cites Plotinus (the founder of Neoplatonism, a Platonic system of philosophy current around 300 AD) in describing the soul as a center, and the need for the sense based or sensible man aware only of complexes in the ego to become unified or one with it:

> It circles around something interior, around a centre. Now the centre is that from which proceeds the circle, that is, the soul. The soul will therefore move around the centre, around the principle from which she proceeds….Anyone who withdraws from it is a man who has remained un-unified, or who is a brute. (p. 219)

Withdrawing from or remaining unconscious of soul prevents human development, because the unity of the transcendent sphere and Self remains unavailable to that person.

The Self is not an archetype, like Plato's One is not a Form. Similarly, the Self exists in the archetypal world like the One exists in the intelligible world, the Self "differs from other ideas [archetypes] …in that it occupies a central position befitting the significance of its content and numinosity" (Jung 1971, 461). Jung defines the Self as "the totality of the conscious and unconscious psyche" (1970, 110), clearly beyond the identity of the archetype. This follows Plato's One, which is beyond the Form, existing as the totality of the material or sense world together with the immaterial or intelligible world (the material world corresponding to consciousness in Jung's nomenclature and the immaterial world to the unconscious). Jung says the Self as the totality contains the "experienceable and the inexperienceable (or the not yet experienced)" (1971, 460).

As the center and source of all life the Self and the One exert a fundamental influence upon the nature of human being. Jung declares, "the Self rules the whole of the psyche" (1976, 731). The Self is a formative power whether a person is aware of it or not causing Jung to declare "the 'giver' of all…things dwells within us" (Jung 1969b, 513). Plato's One is also the formative power in the cosmology, providing the essential unity that holds the universe and the human being together. The power of the Self and One is the glue that contains and integrates the all. Both have a distinct objective life and emanate a cosmic and psychic structure that reflects the law of hierarchical Being, and both create the dual-unity that allows for individuality within utter unity or totality. This cosmic and psychic life is hidden to human awareness until discovered through individuation or the life of philosophy. Both are developmental or growth processes that directly express the formative power of the Self or One. This force or formative power is an inborn urge within each person to grow along a unique path and develop a unique life. Without direct effort, developing a conscious connection between the parts of the psyche and the realms of being is difficult to establish and impossible to stabilize or realize on a permanent basis. Jung reminds us of the challenges involved in making the Self conscious when he remarks: "the self has as much to do with the ego as the sun with the earth. They are not interchangeable" (1966, 238).

The individual who becomes aware of soul circles into some proximity to the Self and One at the center of the psycho-spiritual cosmos and achieves some degree of knowledge of all the worlds through the dual-unity of the cosmic spheres. Jung bridges the gap between worlds by uniting the opposites and making the unconscious conscious. This act connects separate parts and levels of being without sacrificing any part. This idea of bridging the gap between worlds echoes Plato's philosophy, that strives to consciously master the appetites and passions of our sensible nature in order to become aware of the rational soul that unites all the realms. It is a process of realization or knowledge. For Plato and for Jung realizing the hierarchies of worlds defines a condition of being for the human individual; it is a state of wisdom, which is intimacy with the divine One in Plato, and the divine Self in Jung.

Parts of the Whole

In both Plato and Jung a person searching for and achieving this wisdom (experience and knowledge of the next higher level that may lead ultimately to knowledge of the One or Self) does not become identical with the One or Self at the center. It seems there is a cosmic law of hierarchical being that protects individuality. Although a person becomes entirely unified with the Self or One, he or she is not merged completely in the divine. Through states of dual-unity such an awareness of unity may be fully realized and communicated in their individuality. By uniting the realms of being psychically and cosmically, the individual has become conscious in the "two-as-one," or the dual-unity of same and different, part and whole, one and many. Thus participating in the wisdom of the cosmic sphere, an individual has reached a degree of subtlety that is unity with the One with only the thinnest veil of separation. The rare soul able to achieve this level of proximity to the divine One or Self is not destroyed in the totality of God. Rather, this conscious individual is a fully actualized being *in relation* to the whole or God: the part related to the whole of the One or the Self. This conscious wholeness is a path leading into infinity, an ever-increasing subtlety of experience of the divine One or Self.

Journeying towards knowledge of the One in Plato means developing awareness of the immaterial world and bringing it into material existence. The same is true in Jung where in order to experience knowledge of the Self one must develop awareness of the unconscious world and bring it into consciousness. The unknown substance of the hidden realm becomes known, thereby linking the two worlds. In Plato it is called immaterial substance and in Jung it is called psychoid substance, a topic I revisit beginning on page 161. In my experience it seems that this unknown substance originates in higher realms and when it becomes conscious, it subtilizes (makes more subtle) physical perception, eventually opening up conscious experience of an immaterial world.

Plato's One and Jung's Self share the same fundamental meaning or ultimate purpose in human life, which is to draw consciousness towards divine unity in order to realize it. Both the One and the Self are the source of an irresistible and magnetic force that draws a person towards this experience of wholeness, even though the process may remain out of the person's awareness. This draw or magnetic force is an insistent call "home." Mentioned earlier, this force is teleological according to both Plato and Jung, and it refers to the natural developmental urge in human life that prompts us to find an ever-deepening interior world and, eventually, our own source of life.

Seeking the interior world and eventually the One or Self appears as many different desires in accord with the current level of a person's being in both Plato and Jung. These desires are a condition of mind, and they attract certain objects and events in a life space that forms a personal path. Long periods of time (lifetimes according to Plato) are spent on desires pertaining to appetite and spirit, or on the complex and ego in Jung. Once a certain level of growth has been reached the desire that appears and magnetizes attention in both systems is a desire for consciousness and interior awareness. Plato called this the rational and Jung referred to it as a desire for integration and balance. Attempting to satisfy the desire for consciousness leads inward to the mystery of the One and Self.

The supreme One in Plato and the transcendent and immanent Self in Jung remain the central longing of the human individual even prior to the overt stage of desiring consciousness. Before desiring consciousness, people are unconscious of the force sustaining them and are led forward according to their level of being. At every stage of development one is drawn to their center through what is personally meaningful or desirable. Until the person reaches the desire for consciousness, the good of the One or Self is refracted through the level of being of that person, appearing in the guise of activity, experience, goods, and other things that are immediately valued. The level of being concerning egocentric affairs is associated with the degree of injury and wounding sustained by the ego—and maintained by the complexes. The greater the injury and wounding, the further away will be a healthy or integrated complex and therefore healthy ego experience and the center of being in the Self or the One.

The distant truth of the Self and the One is translated to the individual level of being in the ego in a manner that is perfectly tailored to attract and bring that person forward in the now. In this way, a person is always drawn forward to the good of the Self or the One. As a person grows, the "experience near" or immediate desire that draws a person forward gets closer and closer to the center or truth, which then appears at the center of ordinary activity, experience, and even goods.

Since the One and the Self inform all other ontological levels, they create and sustain the whole world. Giving everything existence, they draw all creation towards transformation in the work of return to unity. The process of becoming that level of unity is what we refer to as life. Even those involved in what seem to be the most destructive of ego-laden activities are still engaged in this journey. They provoke or cause what seem to be destructive experiences because they are unconscious of their center or source of being so are unaware of themselves on deeper levels. Destructive forces unleashed in the psyche and therefore in life, and the suffering that ensues, are what compel a human to awaken. Therefore, one can understand that the shadow, as Jung calls it, is included in the divine Self or God. In the same vein, Plato speaks of time spent on appetite and passion as a necessary preliminary to wisdom. Later I will examine in more detail the path of the individual towards wholeness when I explore transformation in individuation and philosophy.

The next level of being descending from the One or Self is the intellect or intelligible world of Form in Plato, and the archetypes or the archetypal world in Jung. Let's proceed and examine the similarities between these two worlds.

The Form and the Archetype

The Form

In Plato the essential Forms of the intelligible realm are "exhibited" by the One. They are a unity or undifferentiated multiplicity of divine, living beings revolving around their origin, the One. The intelligible realm *is* the Forms since they are simultaneously a whole and a part, unified so they can't be separated, as well as differentiated so they are also parts. As parts of the whole, each Form is composed of two factors, the One and itself. The part or form creates a plurality (Taylor 1960, 68), a world beyond the One. Plato calls this interrelationship of part and whole the Indefinite Dyad, or the One and Many. The One gives the Forms their transcendence and unity, as well as knowledge about each other. The many refers to each particular Form and their differences.

Forms transcend the sensible world. They are objective realities, in other words, they exist by themselves as an object (objective reality) outside our subjective experience. Participating in and thereby defining the sensory or sensible world of particulars, Forms become human thought, concept, and discourse. They are objects of thought that not only occupy the mind but also define a subjective state of being. They are not just a rational thought or a concept, because as a living being, they affect the human spirit as a state or feeling tone. However, without the Forms, human thought and feeling would have no content and there would be no personal communication. In *The Sophist*, Plato (1961, 1007) says, "Any discourse we can have owes its existence to the weaving together of forms."

Plato asserts that forms participate in the particulars of sense based or sensible reality as Form copies or images. This means that when the Forms are expressed in sensible reality they are no longer their original being. Instead, the Forms are copies or images of that form. In the *Phaedo,* Plato writes about the forms as causes: "A thing can be said to be something and to deserve the name that we apply to it only in virtue of its participation in a particular Form. In that sense the form is the 'cause' of its existence" (Bluck 1955, 17). The Form copy participates in the original Form and is perceived as the sensible particular with a name. Ontologically, Forms are real in the intelligible world and their images, which inform sensible reality (the world of becoming or physical reality), depend entirely upon them.

A Form never changes its identity in the intelligible world. In the concrete world a particular artifact or experience, "something with a name," participates in a single Form; opposite forms do not appear together. For example, something may be hot, and in order for it to become cold, the hot must withdraw by degrees or perish for the cold to be admitted. Through participation, Forms give everything in the physical world substance, quality, and character. They "enter and depart from this receptacle" (Plato 1996, vol. II, 452) as a Form copy. The Form copy is in relation to the form like an image in a mirror. The copy is not just a likeness of the original; it is derived from it. The image depends on the original; the original does not depend on the image. Interpenetrating and pervasive "by reason of their communion with actions and bodies and each other, they [the Forms] appear everywhere, and each appears as many" (Rowe 1984, 65). Forms also cause action: "Everything an object is or does will be the result of its participation in some form or forms" (Bluck 1955, 24). They are everywhere and many because an idea (form) is "like one and the same day, which is in many places at the same time and nevertheless is not separate from itself (Raven 1965, 212).

Informing and bringing the physical world alive, like the undivided light of the sun, Forms are whole in their own world yet appear in parts in ours. According to everything thus described, one can see that Forms are essential to human life. In both Jung and Plato, Forms or archetypes are perceived according to individual capacity. If a person is unaware, Forms and archetypes are not in experience yet they still constantly inform perception and understanding and therefore growth. Forms are knowledge in Plato's philosophy, so the person who experiences only the image or Form copy of the form in the sensory or sensible realm, or the form itself, experiences different levels of knowledge. Briefly describing the relationship of Forms and knowledge will help deepen our understanding of the intelligible realm of Forms.

In Plato, knowledge is being. In the theory of Forms, real knowledge cannot be taught, it must be revealed and remembered. In *The Euthydemus* (Plato 1961, 409) it is said, "Do you know what you know by something or not? Yes, I said, by the soul." Information can be imparted but truth and understanding can only be experienced and recollected and this happens in the soul. Acquiring truth and understanding in the soul is equated with wisdom, the ultimate state of knowledge. As the soul transforms from lower to higher realms or awareness of the sensory, sensible world to awareness of Forms, knowledge transforms as well. Such transformation involves knowing first, sensual things on earth. Then the soul moves to abstraction, or a knowing of things stripped of their concrete nature. The last stage of knowledge is that of remembering in recollection. This is a comprehending or understanding of things in the simple truth of their intelligible, divine nature through intuition and presence. This is recollection and remembrance because the soul apprehends the nature of the Form rather than the Form copy in its particular. Such is the nature of true intelligence in Plato, and as said earlier, it happens in the soul.

One must begin this process of knowledge with the stimulation of a sense object and work towards realization. Socrates says in the *Phaedrus*:

> Man must attain to understanding by way of a generic concept expressed in words, resulting from many acts of sense-perception, formed into a unity by means of reflection; and this is a recollecting of those things which our soul once beheld. (Bluck 1955, 147)

The repetition of sense experience leads to reflection, which is a symbolizing and abstraction of the earlier concrete experience. The unifying of many sense experiences in abstraction and symbol is a reflection that becomes recollection because reflection is a mirror for the Form above. Levels of knowledge and their relation to the Forms are described in Plato's celebrated divided line allegory. Each section of line in the allegory is defined by a state of being that is shaped by its corresponding object of knowledge. The top two sections of the divided line exist in the world of Forms and the bottom two in the world of visible things. In the bottom two, knowledge is shaped through perception of the Form copy image rather than the Form itself. In this state they remain uncoordinated. In the upper two, the Forms are coordinated, brought together, and apprehended in their true light as a whole.

The lower two sections of the divided line relate to the visible world and describe states of opinion, or *doxa*. These are belief (*pistis*), or even lower, the state of illusion (*eikasia*). Illusion is produced in conjecture, confusion, and befuddlement stemming from perceiving images (form copies) in shadows and reflections of Form copies, not even the form copy itself. This level of knowledge, the illusion of opinion based on shadows of images, concerns the dimmest perception of reality and I will relate it later to Jung's shadow, or perceiving life through the shadow or images that are unconscious projections of emotionally laden and unresolved conflicts. Belief is a higher state than illusion but still that of opinion. It is the result of perceiving the images (still form copies) of physical things themselves as they appear in animals, plants, and the artifacts of the world. Perceiving the images of physical things in the world allows for belief based on observations but still prevents knowledge from being properly ordered and also allows perceptions to be constantly changing.

The two higher sections, *dianoia* and *noesis*, are where true knowledge begins in the realization of the Forms, which can only be apprehended in the soul. *Dianoia* admits of ideas themselves, hypothesis based in science and mathematical and deductive reasoning always aimed at higher principles like the truth. *Noesis* is the highest state of knowing. Reached through dialectic, which is contemplation, it is a state of understanding. *Noesis* is a level of knowledge representing intuition and presence to the Forms as well as to the first principle the One or Good. It is the soul's ultimate realization of the One.

The development of knowledge is equated with the development from sense to soul, and to the soul's ability to become conscious or present to the level of Forms in the intelligible realm. On the bottom two levels of knowledge, belief and opinion, the soul is persisting in the illusions of the sensory or sensible world. This concrete world of particulars is located below the soul on the ontological hierarchy of being. Although originating from the intelligible sphere of Forms, the sensory or sensible world is cast in a very different mold, that of necessity in the realm of mutable, composite, and destructible conditions. It differs specifically from the world of forms in that it is principally the realm of becoming rather than of being. Becoming in the realm of the sensible and concrete was for Plato a world of appearances, a world he usually referred to as nonbeing. This world exists only in relation to the eternal, intelligible world of Forms, the world of real being.

One must transcend the concrete world according to Plato in order to reach the world of real being in the intelligible world of Form. Doing this implies the ability to achieve a unity in the rational aspect of soul rather than being divided into the oppositions of the passions and appetites. In Jung, it means the ability to achieve a unity in the developed soul instead of living in the conflicts and oppositions of the ego. This ability to achieve unity within is a prerequisite or necessary task in both Plato and Jung in order to realize being and knowledge in Form and archetype. We will discuss this at length when looking at individuation and philosophy later on.

The Archetype

Plato's theory of forms and the intelligible realm is reflected in many respects in Jung's psychology. Jung makes direct reference to this debt in several places throughout the *Collected Works*. In the *Archetypes and the Collective Unconscious* Jung acknowledges the Platonic roots of the archetype:

> In the products of fantasy the primordial images are made visible and it is here that the concept of the archetype finds its specific application. I do not claim to have been the first to point out this fact. The honor belongs to Plato. (Jung 1968a, 78-79)

Referring to the Platonic Form in its eternal, transcendent, and even supercelestial nature, Jung declares much earlier in this same text, "The word 'idea.' It goes back to…Plato, and the eternal ideas are primordial images stored up…in a supercelestial place as eternal, transcendent forms" (1968a, 33). Later on he says, "There are present in every psyche forms which are unconscious but nonetheless active—living dispositions, ideas in the Platonic sense, that perform and continually influence our thoughts and feelings and actions" (79).

Jung defers directly to Plato in describing the archetypes. They are "universal dispositions of the mind, and they are to be understood as analogous to Plato's forms (*eidola*) in accordance with which the mind organizes its contents" (Jung 1969b, 517). They "exist almost everywhere and at all times…" (7). In *Mysterium Coniunctionis* Jung (1970) remarks "it [the collective unconscious] takes the place of the Platonic realm of eternal ideas." Both realms, the collective unconscious and the intelligible realm, are objective, *a priori*, universal categories of being. Jung's archetypal world is collective because it is "identical in all individuals (1968a, 43) and is "the prior condition of [man's] experience" (Jung 1966, 95). It "forms the basis of every personality" (148), and is "the source of the instinctual forces of the psyche and of the forms or categories that regulate them, namely the archetypes" (1969c, 158). In the collective unconscious or archetypal world archetypes are "mutually contaminated to such a degree that they cannot be distinguished from one another…everything is connected to everything else" (1970, 462-463). As a unified whole the collective unconscious is also each archetype, "a dynamic image, a fragment of the objective psyche" (1966, 109). As early on as *The Psychogenesis of Mental Disease*, Jung formulates the Platonic basis of the archetype when he considers "the logic of the intellect, the *raison du coeur*, the emotions, the instincts, the basic images and forms of imagination, have in a way more resemblance to…Plato's *eida* than to…our personal minds" (1960, 243).

Through Jung's own words, we can establish the origin of the archetype in Plato's Form. It is a primordial image, eternal, transcendent, a super-celestial Form, a living disposition of the mind, and the intellect, emotion, instinct, and imagination. Like Plato who said that a Form was every determinant of mind and experience, Jung identifies every psychic event and experience as "deeply grounded in the archetype and are so much interwoven with it…" (Jung 1969b, 89). The archetype is "Plato's conception of the Idea as supraordinate and pre-existent to all phenomena" (1968a, 75). It is "far from being a modern term, [it] was already in use before the time of St. Augustine, and was synonymous with the 'Idea' in the Platonic usage" (p. 75).

As a spiritual realm the collective unconscious has the same level of knowledge as Plato's intelligible world. It "contains a superior analysis or insight or knowledge which consciousness has not been able to produce" (Jung 1969b, 41). The collective unconscious is "vastly superior to the life of nature" (1968a, 210), "higher than consciousness" (1967b, 430), and "all pervading, omnipresent, omniscient spirit…an extension of man beyond himself" (1970, 10). The realization of this spiritual unconscious is a "rebirth in a new dimension" (p. 10), and "an interior spiritual world whose existence we never suspected" (1966, 77).

Jung identifies his psychology with a return to Platonic metaphysics and the corresponding resurgence of the spirit in human empirical or sense-based experience:

Anyone who continues to think as Plato did must pay for his anachronism by seeing the "supercelestial," i.e., metaphysical, essence of the Idea relegated to the unverifiable realm of faith and superstition, or charitably left to the poet. Once again, in the age-old controversy over universals, the nominalist standpoint has triumphed over the realistic, and the Idea evaporated …Since that time the Idea is no longer something *a priori*, but is secondary and in our own day signs foreshadowing a change of attitude are rapidly increasing.…pave[ing] the way for a rebirth of the Platonic spirit. If it be true that there can be no metaphysics transcending human reason, it is no less true that … [there is] an *a priori* structure of cognition.…thinking, understanding, and reasoning …are *psychic functions*… Today we are convinced that…psychological premises exist… (Jung 1968a, 76-77)

Jung's psychic premise is his archetype, which corresponds to Plato's pre-existent, *a priori* form. Both function as a transcendent structure of the psyche that determines inner experience as well as perception of objective, external reality.

The archetype expresses the "high value" of transmitting metaphysical experience into empirical life. It does this as a "metaphysical idea, paradigm or model in a transcendent realm, while real things are held to be only the copies of these models" (Jung 1969c, 135). The archetype has a dual nature like the Platonic Form. It exists on its own in one realm and is altered when expressed in another. The archetype is "an unconscious content that is altered by becoming conscious and by being perceived, and it takes its color from the individual consciousness…" (Jung 1968a, 5).

It takes its color from the individual consciousness because a sensible man living only in the ego shaped by complexes must follow his or her own teleological path towards unity. This path is personal, so internal images are perceived according to level of being, or what desires and dynamics happen to be shaping current experience. Images and reality are influenced by a person's state of mind or being. Anyone practicing psychotherapy has experienced how an individual living very distant from his or her center distorts reality in order to assimilate it. Most people perceive what we refer to as consensual reality (the outer world), yet a sage once remarked that one event has a thousand faces. Such a comment reflects the truth of how the archetype or Form is mirrored in the individual psyche according to how the image reflects his or her own state of being. As one gets closer to the center or whole of the Self, one's awareness mirrors more perfectly the actual archetype itself and therefore the individual "colors" it in lesser and lesser degrees. This paradoxically brings individuality and intimacy with the divine into experience in soul, because of the felt experience of the transcendent archetypal world. At the same time, without sacrificing any vitality of experience in the ego, a space and detachment are introduced that produces a sense of freedom in all levels of awareness.

Jung (1969c, 326) and Plato both considered the archetype and idea a living being. In *Psychology and Alchemy* Jung equates the Lapis (which is the successful alchemical transformation of matter into its highest form) as "living being," to the archetype of the Self (1968b, 118). Both the Lapis and the Self refer to the center or highest level of being that can be achieved through the transformations of human growth. The archetype of the Self is at the center of every other archetype, and all archetypes with their center are "living psychic forces that demand to be taken seriously" (Jung 1968a, 156). They are "unknowable . . . living things, changing their name and guise in never-ending succession . . . disclosing their hidden nucleus by perpetually circumambulating round it" (1969a, 182). This movement of the archetype around the center or Self echoes the circularity of Plato's cosmos. Jung's statement that the archetype is unknowable is contradictory to his attitude about individuation and the mission to realize the Self, which is within the archetypal world. The archetype is unknowable by the empirical personality, but it is knowable through the psycho-spiritual reality of soul.

In *Symbols of Transformation* Jung says the archetypes are "personal agencies . . . [and] felt as actual experiences" (Jung 1967b, 255). They are not only living beings and personal agencies but also Gods and living water:

> Rediscover the Gods as psychic factors, that is, as archetypes of the unconscious… [they are] spirit from above. …Our unconscious hides living water, spirit that has become nature. …Our concern with the unconscious has become a vital question for us—a question of spiritual being or non-being. (1959/1968, 23-24)

Jung equates the archetypes with living Gods because the archetypes possess spiritual being or divine energy. "Thus the 'living idea' is always perfect and always numinous" (Jung 1970, 524). This reference in Jung to perfection reflects Plato's idea of perfection in the One and the Form. The One or Good when it descends into the intelligible world of Forms is perfect in its original being, as is the Self when it descends into the archetypes. An archetype exists as a perfect whole in unity with all other archetypes in a "psychic matrix" (1969a, 182). In its state of unity and also in individual expression, the archetype is numinous as well as perfect. As mentioned before, numinous refers to a holy light characteristic of perfect divinity.

Perfection and wholeness of the Self/One and the intelligible world/archetypal world represent the highest value in Jung and Plato. Perfection inheres in the archetype because like Plato's Form coming from the One, it originates in a state of pure light from the Self. Wholeness according to Jung means an original light, which he calls the archetypal light (Jung 1976, 667). This is the divinity expressed in the God-image of the archetype of the Self, which is part of every archetype. It descends into human experience and presents the individual with the challenges of individuation, or conscious ascent to a state of unity beyond the opposites.

Descending into the lower spheres of personality and the sense based, sensible world, the archetype becomes bipolar (Jung 1968a, 183), meaning its opposite sides are experienced separately. Plato borrowed from the Ephesian philosopher Heraclitus the doctrine of opposites. This doctrine defined the world as made up of opposing forces. These opposing forces create a tension that is held together by the unity of the divine One. Like Plato, Jung describes the natural world as defined by opposites, which had to be separated in order to come together again in conscious unity. Fluctuation between the opposites is as natural in the complex and therefore ego, as it is in the sensible man. Both Plato and Jung build into their systems a teleological urge that calls a person to work towards unity of opposites, fulfillment of the spirit, and the experience of transcendent wholeness. The perfection/wholeness inherent in the archetype and Self draws an individual towards the higher realms of consciousness.

An important difference between Jung and Plato concerning perfection and wholeness has to do with the opposite or antithesis of evil. Evil (referred to as shadow in Jung and nonbeing in Plato) means different things in the two systems. According to Plato evil or vice is the result of the last and dimmest hypostasis of creation (the sense based or sensible world), which is the shifting, changing illusion and belief belonging to states of becoming or non-being. Jung calls it the shadow and it pertains to everything people are not conscious of that shapes experience. Evil for Jung is a vital and necessary force of being, because it is only by becoming conscious of the shadow that integration and growth of soul can occur. For Jung, darkness, evil, or shadow is mutual to the highest value found in the Self and its matrix, the collective unconscious. "Like God the unconscious has two aspects; one, good, favorable, beneficent. The other evil, malevolent, disastrous" (Jung 1967, 682). In spite of this important difference, non-being in Plato and the shadow for Jung are dealt with similarly in that both need to be mastered in order to transcend to awareness of the archetype and Form.

With Jung and Plato, divine energy in Form and archetype are expressed similarly. In Plato the Form is called luminous because it is made of light. Jung (1969c, 104) calls it *numinosum*, a term he borrowed from Rudolf Otto. Numinous has a complex meaning denoting "holy," which includes the "archetypal light" of the God-image or archetype of the Self. It also includes the highest moral good and a quality of the sacred that is "irreducible." Numinous and luminous have to do with the divine influx of the higher spiritual world conducted through the archetype or form.

Jung refers to the pure Form of world soul and its fiery sparks, which he asserts "correspond to the Platonic Ideas, from which one could equate the [sparks] with the archetypes…[they] have about them a certain effulgence…[their] numinosity entails luminosity" (Jung

1969c, 191). This magnetic light or the luminous numinosity of the archetype has a certain attraction that links the two realms of archetype and ego complex together in dual-unity within the psyche, even when outside awareness. Jung (1967b, 294) explains: "Since this archetype is numinous, i.e., possesses a specific energy, it will attract to itself the contents of consciousness." Jung refers to this specific energy of the numinosum as exerting a teleological pull: "The archetype has a numinous character: it exerts a fascination, it enters into active opposition to the conscious mind" (pp. 308-309). This pull of the opposites (active opposition or complement) leads a person to the efforts of individuation or wholeness, through which opposites are recognized and integrated. Contents of consciousness and the archetype are then felt together in some degree of realization.

The Image

For both Plato and Jung the image and Form copy inherently link the original Form and archetype to the sensory/sensible man and the ego and its complexes. Also, the conflicts or opposites of these lower realms must be mastered in order to experience higher consciousness in soul. In the philosophy and psychology the luminous, numinous, divine energy of the archetype and Form are of the highest value, sustain all life, contain and express the highest value to lower levels of the cosmology, and also draw an individual towards developing consciousness.

Both Plato and Jung considered the archetype and Form spiritual organs because they function in these vital ways, conducting all aspects of life force to the individual. In Plato the Form is the organ that conducts divine energy or light (consciousness) into human experience. Identical to this, the archetype is "a psychic organ . . . an element of our psychic structure . . . the real but invisible roots of consciousness" (Jung 1968a, 160). As psychic organ both archetype and Form receive and conduct being from a metaphysical realm into sense based, sensible, empirical reality. Plato describes this process in his line and cave allegories. Both allegories portray conditions that shape perceived reality. I have described the line allegory earlier, and will connect the cave allegory in this respect in this section and describe it fully in the chapter on soul.

It is worth exploring the depth and complexity of what image means for Plato and Jung as it is a central attribute of all the archetypes and Forms. The psyche is an expression and experience of images, in both the philosophy and psychology. Jung describes that images expressed through the "organ of the psyche…deal with categories of the imagination which is why…I call them archetypes" (Jung 1969b, 518). The archetype and the Form are a whole realm of interpenetrated, substantial living beings, each a living image that can only be felt and known through the corresponding counterparts that are radiated into the lower level of reality in sensible man in Plato and the ego and its complexes in Jung.

I believe that Plato would agree with Jung that human experience is "a complicated structure of mental images" (1969c, 327). Each structure is an archetype or Form reflected in an image, called symbol in Jung and form copy in Plato, experienced within the ego complex consciousness or sensory/sensible man. Personal perception is determined by images outside the self at first, and as development proceeds the image or form copy is also perceived from within the interior psyche, differentiated from the outer image. The image reflected from the intelligible realm and the archetypal collective unconscious remain whole in their own realm while being perceived as a part from either without or within until the opposites are integrated. In this way, the Form and archetype give life and knowledge a continuous unity even when held as opposites within the psyche, in separate, individual consciousness. Therefore, their wholeness paradoxically supports our separate sense of ego/self while being the unifying force that holds the world and human reality together.

The image reflected in perception is a symbolic event even if a person is unaware of the nature of perception. In other words, a person who understands images as literal or concrete pictures coming from the outside world is not aware of the symbol. Science tells us that photons of light, not a picture, enter the eye. Images are generated from the mind and although it appears as if they originate externally and are impressed upon the eye it is the other way around: the image originates in a symbol reflected from deeper within (or above) from the intelligible realm and is projected outward. In Plato, the symbolizing process begins in hypostasis where one level of reality appears or is symbolized in another. This is also true in Jung's psychology, where one level of reality appears or is symbolized in another. Jung says apprehending the image is a "symbolic process [that] is an experience *in image and of images*" (Jung 1968a, 38). In spite of the general human proclivity to perceive only the literal level of the image, the symbolic can be discovered in the interior psyche and also the original archetype can be felt through the intangible numinosity or divinity associated with it.

Unlike Plato who does not assign value to the images of Form copies and shadows, Jung values all levels of the image. He remarks in the *Structure and Dynamics of the Psyche*, "The shadows on the wall of Plato's cave are just as real as the invisible figures that cast them, and whose existence can only be inferred mathematically (1969c, 213).

Plato's cave allegory describes how reality is defined by the way an image is perceived, and how this happens according to level of being. I will describe this allegory at length in the section on Plato's soul: briefly the allegory is about how people's usual level of being keeps them living in chains, meaning a very limited capacity to perceive reality. These people can see images on the wall of the cave as they pass between the wall and the fire, but the images are only shadows, not the real world. By becoming unchained, people can perceive the image in themselves rather than in reflection on the wall. Eventually, they are exposed to conditions such as the light, which represents higher knowledge. Such steps in perception are at first painful and difficult as adjustments must be made in order to admit experience of higher realities.

It seems that Jung would understand the shadows in the cave as having value in spite of being projected onto the wall, although lesser value than the interior psychic image or the archetypal image. It is of lesser value in a Jungian perspective because as a projected image, the person has a more circumscribed perception of reality due to his or her undeveloped mind. The mind can be improved and perception clarified through individuation, which brings the opposites together and thereby renders projection unnecessary, although it still occurs in a benign way. For Plato, the shadow on the wall has no value because it has no real being, so a person must expend effort to transcend it by learning philosophy.

Like Plato's Form copy, which is a reflected image of the Form, the symbol in Jung is a reflected image of the archetype. Both Form and archetype are blueprints upon which all empirical or external experience is fashioned. Jung refers to this when he says, "The greatest and best thoughts of man shape themselves upon these primordial images as upon a blueprint" (1966, 69). All thought, feeling, etc., is based on the primordial archetype, translated to the symbol within, which is projected outward in image that provides the foundation for all perception and experience. The archetype or image includes feelings because an image is as much feeling as thought. Jung (1976, 257) describes that the image is "connected with the living individual by the bridge of emotion" because desire or emotion shape thought.

With Plato and Jung, the image is conditioned by whether a person is able to apprehend only the external, projected image, or the shadow of the Form copy, versus an interior symbol or Form copy, or the Form or archetype itself. The state of a person's consciousness thus defines how reality is perceived. In Jung's psychology reality can be apprehended in a spectrum between the lowest level of perception in the bi-ologic instinct in matter (Jung 1968a, 44), and the highest level in the spiritual and transcendent realms. The spectrum manifests in colors, with the biologic/instinct being red and the spiritual realm being violet. In Plato's scheme, images are also conditioned according to where a person's consciousness exists in a spectrum of reality. Plato's spectrum has as its highest level the Good (God or the One, commensurate with Jung's violet level) to the lowest end of the spectrum in the sense based or sensible world of particulars found in physical matter (Jung's red).

On this spectrum of reality, Jung identifies specific inner images that are also events or categories of experience like marriage or death, and figures such as the object-imago (caretaker other), shadow, the child, the wise man, the mother, trickster, and anima/animus that can be realized within and made conscious. Experiencing the numinous or divine aspect of these images and figures means perceiving the arche-type at the highest end of the spectrum, while experiencing the figures as images externally means perceiving the biologic, red, lower end of the spectrum. Most people are in between the highest or purest expe-rience of the transcendent, and the lowest and most limited experience of the concrete, thereby having a mix of outer and inner experience. Those with a closer proximity to the transcendent are more influenced by inner experience and those closer in degree to the instinctual and concrete are more influenced by outer experience without modification by inner reflection.

Plato divides experience and therefore image into type or category a bit differently, specifying the appetites, passions, the spirited and the rational aspects of the self or soul. The nature of each of these categories of image and experience organizes and conditions a person's state of mind and his or her conflicts. A person's experience *reflects* the condi-tion of their mind, which consists of an image and its meaning, On every level from lowest to highest, personal reality is governed by the image. Jung says it succinctly:

Consciousness has no direct relation to any material objects. We perceive nothing but images, transmitted to us…Between the nerve-endings of the sense-organs and the image that appears in consciousness, there is interpolated an unconscious process which transforms the physical fact of light, for example, into the psychic image "light.".…The consequence of this is, that what appears to us as immediate reality consists of carefully processed images, and that, furthermore, we live…in a world of images. (1969c, 383-384)

Since we live completely in a world of images supplied only by the psyche, it is therefore these images alone that make any knowledge of objects possible. In Jung's psychology the complexes that inform ego experience (in opposition and in degrees of integration) condition the images of reality that lead to knowledge and understanding of self and world. A more integrated complex leads to increased understanding, an interior symbol or image, and eventually the felt numinosity of the archetype. This integration brings along with it an increased understanding of the ego's experience. A higher reality as well as a higher knowledge belongs to the person who has this level of development.

Jung's psychology of being and knowledge follows Plato's theory of knowledge in recollection (discussed earlier in the line allegory) where a person's level of being (degree or depth of awareness one has achieved) is equal to the degree of presence he or she has been able to realize in the image. A person realizes more presence in the image to the degree he or she is able to experience it internally rather than externally. Perceiving the form copy, a person is experiencing the external image only and does not notice an interior image or state with it. Perceiving on a less concrete level, a person is aware of the outer image and also apprehends an internal image or symbol, which is also a state of being and may be felt within consciously. On a yet more integrated level of perception, experience goes beyond perceiving the form copy and interior image/symbol or state by including a transcendent feeling, which is a state of being that is connected to the Form itself. In this state, one has achieved knowledge of the deepest realities by apprehending the numinous archetypal image with the One within it. Perception of the image at this stage includes the whole as well as the part because all of the levels of reality are held within the felt experience of the Form or archetype itself and the One or Self within it. Therefore, it can be understood that in both Plato and Jung, the image itself opens up deeper worlds depending on level of being in perception.

To say it another way, perception of an image changes as one achieves deeper awareness of symbolic, archetypal, and divine realities. As one moves from the concrete, sense based/sensible or literal world of images into a more interior and symbolic understanding, the image transmits to the perceiver an interior world of meaning that exists separate from "outer" influences. The image therefore transmits not only the outer form and its consensual meanings, but also an inner meaning that does not depend on the immediate outer sensing of the world. Deepening this perception of the symbolic understanding of the image into realization of the archetype and the One or Self (that is always informing every image whether one knows it or not) brings what I call an in-breathing of a numinous sense of being. This capacity occurs due to the person's ability to feel and "see" or understand the transcendent, living light that coheres and brings life into the immanent image. This light is sourced from the archetype or Form within the psyche.

I use the term in-breathing when describing the changes of perception that occur when one reaches the level of being represented by feeling the archetype or Form, and thus Self and One, because it reflects the traditional wisdom that this deeper realm is actually "closer than one's breath." Learning to exist in proximity to the archetypal realm begins like all growth, in bits and spurts, and gradually becomes a more stable and intentional state. As this process develops, one actually begins to experience the need for this "breath" or contact with higher being like one needs oxygen. Going without presence to higher being and the archetypal realm at least in my own experience, is a flattening and hollowing out of the world and one's life in it.

The changes wrought in perception of the image when one begins to consciously integrate the dual-unities of the sense based/sensible and ego complex realm with the archetypal image or form and the dimension of the Self/One involve infinite degrees of proximity, meaning there is no limit to how close one can get to the Self/One/God There is a treasure of beautiful mystical literature written throughout the ages elaborating on these experiences for the student of the Self. As my own practice deepens perception of the image, I have experienced the difference between awareness on the personal and collective level versus the individual and archetypal level of being. The former level is ego or complex laden (preoccupied with supporting the ego) and shaped by the collective mind or societal trends. The latter is more individual with some degree of freedom from this central preoccupation and a noticeable need for solitude, which is required for inner realization. The experience of individuality is linked with the archetype directly rather than being influenced by its mirror in the collective culture. When I am in a state of archetypal awareness, I experience the Self or One as a presence radiating in the light of the image, both within and without. This presence has a deep personally individual feel as well as a vast and cosmic side. Along with this experience of presence is a quality of nameless understanding of the absolute unity of life.

This understanding and experience of image translates into a highly attuned intuition. Intuition is a way of knowing that is sensed from within, where presence to the archetype or Form brings into awareness knowledge of others, events, and life in general. Human life in this more illuminated image is felt to be One, and this sense of Oneness encompasses all being including that of our earth. Perception of the archetypal image is a doorway through which untold meaning flows. The key to this meaning is the certain knowledge that everything here on the concrete plane of physical existence is the outer shell of a deeper reality that is vastly rich in comparison. The many meanings experienced in this richer, more unified world are difficult to express in words. Images and metaphor help to express these meanings. For example, like a plant ultimately sustained by the sun above, a soul cannot develop exclusively through contact with material reality, but needs the deep unconscious spirit "within," which also corresponds to the cosmos "above." In my own experience, the archetypal level of the image sometimes brings elevated states into awareness, but more frequently brings a quiet, contemplative connectedness with all life centered in a sense of peace and acceptance. I continue to work towards this calm, contemplative connectedness as a stable state, and hope to be better disposed for elevated states while understanding they are highlights on the journey, but not the journey itself. These experiences are more by grace than mastery (although one could argue mastery is a form of grace), and I believe one is always a beginner on the path towards unity in wholeness, since it is an infinite path.

To briefly sum up, Jung's and Plato's world of image includes all experience in a spectrum from spiritual to the sense based or sensible. Image at the "highest" end of the spectrum *is* and reflects the spiritual reality of the archetypal image or intelligible form and the divine One or Self in the human experience. The sensible realm is on the other end of the spectrum, or "lowest" end of human experience. It is important to note that although there seems to be a value judgment in the use of the spatial metaphors higher and lower, this is a superficial understanding of the usage.

Higher and lower are terms that describe states of the human soul. The soul never entirely exits the bounded nature of creation, even when fully realizing dual-unity with the divine. States of individual soul and the corresponding images that are realized on this spectrum are inclusive rather than exclusive as one advances or climbs "higher" to divine realization. All the stations on the way have their own intrinsic rewards and purpose, and a balanced life is about participating in each level according to its nature. Therefore, the ego and its complexes have a place of value, as well as higher forms of realization. The designations of better and worse, which may be associated with the language of higher and lower, do not apply in an either/or way. Rather one should think of growth and development as always adding an "and," rather than dividing experience into "or," since consciousness of dual-unity is always inclusive of what has come before.

I hope this brief discussion of the image representing different levels of reality and therefore transforming a person's experience according to their level of awareness helps the reader to understand how we live in a world of images supplied by the psyche and that the level upon which the image is perceived informs consciousness. The point of transformation of experience and image is soul. Exploring how Jung used and elaborated on Plato's ideas of soul will help the reader understand how one changes and grows from one realm to another. This change involves movement from the sense based/sensible and physical realm of image and all its associated ways of being, into higher realities.

The level of being concerning sense based/sensible man in Plato and the ego and its complexes in Jung are the outposts from which teleological return to wholeness begins. Whether in the life of the philosophical disciple in the academy of old, or in the contemporary psychological work of individuation in the psychotherapeutic consulting room, or in the less directed journey of life itself, the image perceived in the sensible or sense based, ego complex oriented outer world is where we all start.

The Ego and Sensible Man
A World of Flux Based on the Opposites

The sense based/sensible world of Plato is similar to the Jungian world of ego and its complexes in significant ways. I have already emphasized that both worlds are reflections in image of archetype and

Form. Both Plato and Jung go beyond the world of the senses and the ego complexes in favor of the deeper archetypal and intelligible realities. Plato denies the sensible world any true substance and thus denies it any being, and Jung (1969c, 383-384) reduces the validity of physical or sensible reality when he refers to all reality as a composite of internal images. In both systems, the physical world of sense or ego complex is a world of change based on the flux of the opposites, a doctrine both Plato and Jung admittedly owe to Heraclitus (Jung 1966, 72). Jung echoes his debt to Heraclitus in the *Archetypes and the Collective Unconscious* when he says, "The world exists only because opposing forces are held in equilibrium" (1968, 94). In Plato's sensible world and in Jung's world of ego and complexes a person experiences the impact of physical existence in order to eventually transcend it.

The potentially riotous claims of perceived external stimuli in the sensible or physical world demand reaction and adaptation and therefore shape and form personal consciousness. They usually press upon the adult a need to subsist, meaning at the very least generating enough concentration and organization to feed, clothe, and house the body. Mastery of the outer world and its demands develops concentration, self-control, and attention. These learned attributes combined with temperament whittle consciousness into a unique pattern, which Jung refers to as complexes informing ego experience and Plato refers to as the sensible man. The adaptations required of the developing child are well known to psychologists, and most people also grasp the importance of these fundamental years. Adult adaptation builds upon previously learned schemas and since science has discovered that the brain is plastic, meaning we continue to grow new neural pathways, adulthood continues to be a path of development and change.

Jung said that the first half of life was a time to devote to succeeding in this outer adaptation or development in the sensible or ego/complex world. In the latter half of life, he suggested a person focus on internal realities in preparation for the final adaptations: the losses of elder life that culminate in the ultimate loss of death. In Jung's psychology, conditions from childhood influence and form the complexes that translate as ego experience. In Plato's psychology, the lower nature or the appetites and passions (the passions are referred to as the spirited aspect) influence and form the sensible man's experience. In both the philosophy and psychology, an adult unable to grasp and master either the complexes or the appetites and passions of the sensible world suffer from the constraints of that same world. Such a person struggles and suffers some degree of internal and external chaos, a sense of victimization, and a lack of freedom and autonomy. Usually there is strong affect involved, referred to in Plato as the irrational and in Jung as complexes. In these conditions, the individual is chained to the sensible world or ego and complexes through sudden and sometimes inexplicable reactions. It is the reaction that chains the person, not the outer event.

At some point in time, a person who has developed this outer aspect of being into some kind of adapted, organized stability comes to the realization that there is more to life than what ego and complex or the sense based world offers. Attention is then turned towards the mystery of the inner world, and thus begins another stage of development. This man is "the spiritual man [whose] distinguishing mark…is that he seeks self-knowledge and knowledge of God" (Jung 1967a, 94). In the ancient world it was the man who turned inward towards the study and life of philosophy. When this turning or change occurs, the next level of being (beyond sense and ego/complex) is approached.

In Plato's ancient world the visible, sensible, and finite world is created by a demiurge. A demiurge is a subordinate deity in the Greek pantheon of Gods. The *Timaeus* is Plato's myth of creation and in this dialogue he tells of this demiurge or divine craftsman who crafts the world from a perfect and eternal living model. Since unable to bestow the fullness of ideal or eternal being upon a sensible creature, being was bestowed mathematically in measure or in parts upon a moving image according to number, which we call time (Plato 1961, 1167). This image in time is a part that is also a limit, while the perfect model lives in eternity. It is the imposed limit that allows the power of acting and being acted upon in the world of becoming.

As an image of its eternal model or idea, the sensible world has the same characteristics as its more perfect model, but is a limited or lesser reality. A world of appearance, the sensible realm lacks any true substance or reality because its nature is one of continuous change. In the *Cratylus* (Plato 1961, 473), realness as essence or original form is contrasted with the changing states of becoming. "How can that be a real thing which is never in the same state? For obviously things which are the same cannot change while they remain the same…" In the realm of becoming everything is in a state of flux or constant change while conditions in the eternal world remain the same.

Heraclitus, mentioned earlier, was a philosopher from Ephesus who contributed the idea that opposing forces make up the world. The Logos or divine being holds these two opposing forces together within a unity and this doctrine of opposites is the universal flux of Plato's constantly changing world of sensible reality. "All things are in motion and nothing is in rest; he [Heraclitus] compares them to the stream of a river, and says that you cannot go into the same water twice" (Plato 1961, 439). Plato brought this doctrine of flux into his epistemology (theory of knowledge) when he denied the world of sense any knowledge or being. Things of sense and the world they inhabit are not objects of knowledge because they lack the substance of the eternal, divine ideas or forms. Plato describes in the *Timaeus* different kinds of being:

> One kind of being is the form which is always the same, uncreated and indestructible, never receiving anything into itself from without, nor itself going out to any other, but invisible and imperceptible by any sense, and of which the contemplation is granted to intelligence only. And there is another nature of the same name with it, and like to it, perceived by sense, created, always in motion, becoming in place and again vanishing out of place, which is

apprehended by opinion jointly with sense. And there is a third nature, which is space and is eternal and admits not of destruction and provides a home for all created things…" (p. 1179)

Plato goes on to say that images perceived by sense, and the space or receptacle where images are imprinted, are different from the Forms themselves. The image goes in and out of the receptacle (space) depending on many conditions. Image and space are not unified but remain separate and uncoordinated, apprehended and ruled by the lower sphere of non-being or becoming, and perceived in a "dreamlike sense" (Plato 1961, 1179).

The receptacle or medium in which images appear is referred to as a necessary condition (Cornford 1975, 193). The receptacle, being an unlimited or indefinite substratum (Rowe 1984, 108), is a "universal nature" and is explicitly referred to as "she" in the *Timaeus* (Plato 1961):

Inasmuch as she always receives all things, she never departs at all from her own nature and never…assumes a form like that of any of the things which enter into her; she is the natural recipient of all impressions, and is stirred and informed by them, and appears different from time to time by reason of them. …we have only to conceive of three natures: first, that which is in process of generation; secondly, that in which the generation takes place; and thirdly, that of which the thing generated is a resemblance naturally produced. And may liken the receiving principle to a mother, and the source or spring to a father, and the intermediate nature to a child… (p. 1177)

Space as receptacle in the sensible world is the "nurse, of all generation" (Plato 1961, 1176). It is a pre-cosmic (meaning existing before the creation of reason), eternal, and limiting factor. The receptacle is not an object of rational knowledge (meaning a level of being to aspire to through philosophy) like the Form, nor is it apprehended by the senses. The receptacle is something other. Called the mother, the receptacle is uninformed matter where Form (the father), descends. The in-between existent, the child, is the image or Form copy.

Jung's Ego and Complexes

Jung did not address the nature of the receptacle wherein the image appears in the way Plato addressed this, but nevertheless he made the external world a place where the image is found, as well as defining the psyche as a container and receptacle for images of the archetypal world. He also rooted the ego and its complexes in the world of sense, which is organized by the principle of the opposites originating with Heraclitus and repeated in Plato. In Jung, all phenomena in the world are held together by opposites and this is emphasized in the architecture of the complex, which is bi-polar until unity is achieved through individuation. The ego and the complexes are intrinsically related as together they create personal self-experience before individuation occurs, which lifts consciousness to another level. Complexes form from birth onward, are based on personal experience and are expressed in the ego oriented mostly in the external world since the image is usually found only in the outer world at this stage. They shift and change according to the impact of events. The ego and its complexes are a filter through which a person perceives and translates the meaning of reality. This level of personal experience is also represented in Plato. Called the sensible man it refers to a person perceiving and translating reality through the five physical senses driven by the appetites and irrational desires, and oriented by the external image. Mastering these forces in personal experience through philosophy lifts consciousness to the freedom of the spiritual soul. In both Plato and Jung lifting consciousness above this outermost level of experience involves discovering the internal reality of the image and form.

The opposites within the ego complexes and sensible man's perception give forth images and thus experiences that remain in conflict until a person makes efforts to increase their self-awareness. In Plato, the consequence of suffering and the desire to reduce states of personal conflict sometimes leads to philosophy or the search for wisdom in order to become free from the turmoil. Jung's ego complexes resemble Plato's irrational passions and appetites, as both are conditions of being that keep a person anchored to nothing more substantial than changing perceptions and reactions. I will briefly summarize the psychology of Jung's ego complexes so the reader can more fully understand their nature and function, and how they produce conflicted reactions to external reality. After describing Jung's complexes, I will discuss Plato's sensible world.

Ego and its complexes are developed from birth onwards and organize self-experience. Although Jung's psychological mechanics are more complicated than Plato's, the results are the same: a person perceiving images distant from their intelligible or archetypal source, and remaining in reaction to conflicted and shifting realities that prevent consciousness of higher states of being.

According to Jung, a complex collects around an archetype. Remembering the discussion earlier about image will help the reader understand how the image of the archetype persists unconsciously in the psyche as a symbol within the center of a complex while it exists independently in the archetypal realm. The complex clusters around the image of the archetype, which has its opposite aspect in another complex since the unity of the archetype is bipolar, or separated into opposites in the sense or ego realm. Each complex in consciousness can become unconscious through a different experience. Unconscious complexes do not necessarily have to be negative; sometimes the negative is what is conscious and the positive lurks in the unconscious. An example of a Jungian complex may help. One ego complex Jung identified is the cluster of qualities, attributes, attitudes, experiences, feelings, thoughts, perceptions, and so forth that a person desires to be and thinks they are. An idealized version of the self, Jung called this complex the Persona.

Someone who organizes their sense of self around the persona complex usually remains unaware of the negative unwanted parts of the self. These unwanted parts are relegated to the unconscious, since they are in conflict with the conscious position. Sometimes these repressed or split off parts are put into external reality or other persons. This action of putting unconscious elements of the self into others or the world is called projection. Jung refers to all these rejected aspects of the self as the shadow complex, which is the complementary or opposite complex to the persona. Both are experienced in the ego or the level of the complexes but until integration occurs, they occur singularly as opposites. When the shadow complex becomes more conscious a balance begins to emerge between the persona and shadow, and some degree of wholeness is achieved.

When projected, a complex or parts of a complex remain unintegrated or in opposition. An unintegrated complex is usually experienced through sense-based perception and the internal image is not apprehended. For example, an unconscious aspect of the shadow could be selfishness. When it is projected outward, a person will see the selfishness in someone else. Not realizing the internal image of their own selfishness, this aspect of the shadow will not be integrated with its opposite in the persona, selflessness or generosity. Becoming aware of the opposing internal images of selfishness in the shadow and generosity in the persona deepens awareness into the archetype itself, which holds the opposites of the complexes together in the unity of the archetypal realm (The archetype of the persona and its opposite the shadow become a unity in the archetypal realm). This awareness of unity signifies that the experience of the persona and shadow have been resolved into awareness of soul, which transformation happens in the transcendent function and I will address this further down in the section on the

Transcendent Function. When the opposing complexes have been united through the work of individuation, and the archetype can emerge into awareness, a sense of freedom from the complex expands a person's experience. It is a feeling of wholeness, peace, and unity in the Self. A person has to reintegrate these elements time and again in order to maintain relative freedom from the opposites of the complex. Constant reintegration of these elements is required to achieve unity with the more transcendent wholeness of the archetype, which leads to the felt experience of the Self. The felt experience of the Self goes beyond the image or realization of the archetype.

Another of Jung's complexes experienced in the ego either consciously or unconsciously depending on the level of integration achieved is the object-imago. The archetypes of the object-imago are of caregiving figures, for example the archetype of the mother. The nature of the caretaker, which produces a very personal experience, is an image in the internal world and also an archetype. Archetypes are "an image existing independently of, and yet based on, all perception, and the relative autonomy of the image remains unconscious so long as it coincides with the actual behavior of the object" (Jung 1969c, 274). What this comment means is that archetypes are independent and autonomous yet connected to the image in the personal psyche. When the caretaker other goes against the self, the archetype is activated and the opposing complex (opposed to conscious desire or expectation) emerges. The opposing aspect is projected if the complex is not integrated, and in conscious awareness if it is. If unconscious, the conflict of the opposing image keeps a person in a divided state.

The archetype is whole, having all aspects or images within it, and the complex is not whole until it is integrated and thus able to bring the meaning of the archetype alive. Instead the internal image in the complex usually appears according to a person's consciousness and experience; whatever a person is conscious of in that moment. To clarify further, another example may help. The mother archetype is the unified whole (all created images of mother). This archetypal, internal image at the center of the complex is made of singular images that move in and out of one's experience of being mothered, mostly by the personal mother (father or any other person can be the mother). When the subject begins to experience the object-image or image/experience of the mother different from their need or expectation, some degree of conflict occurs. Two images of the mother are now creating a difficulty in experience. Integrating these two different images of mother means holding both aspects in mind at once. When they remain separate or not integrated (held in mind at once) the opposing aspect may be projected onto another person or group, or even a place.

Withdrawing the projection comes with working through traumas and conflicts thus becoming aware that one's own internal experience has generated the opposing reality (or image), and it is not about someone else, a group, or place, even if there has been an impingement or violation. One doesn't ignore outside factors but in order to maintain one's own inner stability, integration is necessary. In a state of integration, personal experience transcends the opposing images by bringing them together in awareness. This means that one experiences events and others with more autonomy and emotional freedom. One is much less vulnerable to a host of negative associations. Also, being able to find the projection in oneself opens up true relationship with the other.

Another example, mentioned before, is the shadow complex or all those parts of the self one rejects as not good enough. To integrate an aspect of the shadow complex one must become aware of that aspect of the rejected self, through observation and feedback from trusted others, and have the capacity to face the unwanted associated affect, like shame, guilt, and self-hate. Becoming conscious of the negative part of the self brings the projection back into awareness. Integration of the rejected part of a complex (like all integration) is an act of recollection, a collecting back to the self what belongs to it. Recollecting projections is necessary even when the object or event receiving the projection is truly exhibiting some kind of negative or opposing behavior or attitude. There is always a "hook" for a projection, meaning that most projections are placed because there is some stimulus for the placement.

The psychic act of recollection or the withdrawing of a projection back into the self is a result of sophisticated psychological insight, and efforts to master feeling, thought, and behavior. It is a healing act since it unifies the complex, which is necessary in spite of whatever the other person may be doing or saying. It is only through the unification of the opposites in ones own complex that one can understand that the other person is motivated by their own undeveloped and unconscious complexes, and that they are therefore projecting their own inner conflicts. Disagreements that occur without a projected content do not orchestrate conflict in complexes. Instead, such a disagreement is communicated, held between the two persons in a non-threatening way, and resolved with understanding in spite of strong feelings.

One could understand from these descriptions that integration of opposites in complexes allows for knowledge that is also a level of being that reaches beyond the ego's experience of conflicted complexes. Such being allows for understanding and acceptance of the person one is having conflict with: that they themselves are composed of opposing sides, like oneself. The allowance of difference, conflict, and differentiation paradoxically allows for acceptance, a form of unity. Projection of unconscious parts of complexes prohibits differentiation and integration because when a person is relating to a projected part of one's own self, it prevents relationship. A paradox of the dual-unity at the heart of being is that proper differentiation in human relationship occurs only to the degree unity has been achieved within.

As conflicted parts within a complex are incrementally reconnected or united with their opposite content, eventually opposing complexes themselves are connected. All acts of integration herald first a touch and then a more persistent experience of the inner life. First an experience of the image within that forms experience, and then an apprehension of the archetype itself, which brings a numinous sense of unity and understanding. The internal image (the "image" includes thought, feeling, sensation, spirit, in whatever form it occurs) comes into awareness through time and effort spent focusing within one's own self. The external, sense-based image, which is precise and clear and seems to come through the eyes and other senses, has its own beauty, but it represents just the shell of the whole image. When crossing the threshold from perceiving outer images to inner images, one deepens experience beyond the outer shell to include another level of being. Worlds are added at each level of deepening; the inner image moves inward into the archetypal world and then even more deeply inward into unity with the divine Self or One.

Conscious unity among the different self states or parts within is the foundation for coherent inner experience. Another way of understanding this unity is visualizing the separate psychological functions of sense, intellect, feeling, and intuition working in union. Integration of these four psychological functions along with integrations of complexes produces internal awareness.

Plato's Sensible World

In Plato's philosophy, the mechanics of the sense based or sensible man perceiving the outer world are similar in fundamental ways to Jung's ego complexes. The image experienced by the sense-based person in Plato's world also remains external until recollected into an internal experience. Perceiving the Form copy (the image) projected into the external world occurs because the sensible man can react only to the strong appetites, passions, and spirited desires that exist in opposites within, and compel him forward externally without the ability to reflect on them and thus gain self-knowledge.

Like Jung's image in the complex, Plato's Form copy experienced in the sensible world is a shifting spectacle of opposites. A person who decides they want to change the ever-shifting reactions of sensible reality has to focus on educating themselves through philosophy, in order to master the passions and appetites that drive feeling, thought, and behavior. Mastery involves concentrated efforts to contain and balance and therefore unite opposites and resolve conflicts in the lower nature. For example, conflicts and opposites in the lower nature involve the instincts, appetites, and passions, including ambition, greed, strong emotions and habits of thought, feeling, and behavior that produce vice (vice is that which is destructive to balance).

In Plato the rational does not imply rational information but a love of virtue (virtues are attributes of unity and wholeness), and this love translates into a level of being. The force and power of the rational aspect acting on the lower self has the same function that integrating the complexes has in Jung. With both, transcending the conflicts produced by the lower nature leads to a feeling and experience of archetype and Form, and thus the Self and One.

In Plato, Forms in the intelligible world create all experience in the lower nature but the higher rational nature perceives the interior form rather than the Form copy perceived by the sensible man. By mastering the lower sense-based experience with the higher rational nature, the lower man perceiving the Form copy is consciously united with the rational soul and thus able to perceive the higher form. This relationship of dual-unity between higher and lower orchestrates wholeness and balance (or virtue) for the individual. Choosing to develop one's higher nature through philosophy brings the self into balance, unity, and order, which is fashioned after the intelligible world. Proper living according to the virtue learned through philosophy does not imply total abstinence of one's lower nature, but rather each pleasure in appropriate balance. This balance of opposites takes the place of the riotous and irrational lower nature driving desire and impulse, and the various needs of the appetites and passions.

When a person is no longer bound by sense in the outer world in Plato and by ego complexes in Jung, they are no longer only the sensible or ego complex driven man. Internal awareness of the form copy or symbolic image is equated with experience of higher degrees of knowledge, and elevated consciousness and being. This elevated consciousness of being and knowledge is the aim of philosophy, and also the aim of individuation. In Plato it is the soul that unifies and masters the lower with the higher, the appetites and passions with rational being, achieving a conscious, balanced connection or dual-unity among the sense-based external world, the form copy within, and the Form in the intelligible sphere. This is mirrored in Jung where the conscious soul achieves a balanced connection or dual-unity among the externally based and projected image of ego complexes, the internal symbolic image, and the archetype. In both Plato and Jung the sensible world and the world of the ego complex exist in order to develop soul and thereby bring the higher transcendent realm into awareness.

Having described the similarities and even parallels of the Platonic and Jungian cosmos and psyche in the One and the Self, the intelligible and archetypal spheres, and the worlds of sense and ego complex, I will now move on to examine the nature of the individual self as soul in both Plato and Jung.

Chapter Three
Plato's Soul

The eyes of fire that symbolize presence or knowing in the subtle body are a power within thee, in each one of you, that cannot refer to a collective guide … the infinite price attached to spiritual individuality makes it inconceivable that salvation could consist in its absorption into a totality, even a mystical one.
Henry Corbin

Jung developed the concept of the individuated self as soul existing beyond the ego complexes and yet not identical with the archetype and Self. He situated soul in a third ontological category of being: in-between the higher archetype with the Self at its center, and the lower ego complexes associated with the natural world. This arrangement mirrors Plato's development of the individual soul, which he located in-between the Form with the One at its center, and the sensible man in the natural world. Like Plato's self, Jung's true individual self is soul. Soul in the third is disposed to become conscious of relationship with the archetype and Self (Plato's Form and One) at the same time as remaining conscious of the lower ego complexes (Plato's sensible man) through the dynamic of dual-unity. Dual-unity describes both the state of being and the dynamic action of soul in-between in the third where it remains simultaneously in a relationship of duality and unity with both the higher and lower worlds. The dual side of dual-unity refers to the fact that soul is different and separate from both the archetype (with the Self at its center) and the ego complexes. The dynamic of unity makes soul one with these other levels of being.

To my knowledge, Jung's developing the self as individual soul, located ontologically in the third with the dynamic of dual-unity potentially linking all levels of the cosmos and being, has been little examined in Jungian studies. Also unexamined is the engine behind this dynamic: the energetic aspect of the transcendent function which is responsible for transforming consciousness of being from the natural level to soul in the third. Last, Jung's considerations about the soul having a subtle body of immaterial matter have not been linked to the nature of this individual self as soul. I will consider all of these issues in detail but will begin with Plato's soul, so we can see the root of Plato's philosophy of the individual self in Jung.

There has been plenty of scholarly debate on the nature of Plato's soul over the centuries. I intend to summarize the salient features relevant to my argument, relying on diverse sources spanning the contemporary condensed translation of the *Dialogues* by Hamilton and Cairnes, to the lengthy translation of Thomas Taylor (1758-1835), whose work brings the ancient, more esoteric wisdom of Plato into the modern world. These translations have been clarified and buttressed by other scholarly commentaries and reader feedback, in particular from Tim Addey, a Plato scholar from Thomas Taylor's publishing house.

The features I am focusing on are the structure of soul, its immortality, its placement in the third in-between Form and sense, and its dual-unity with other levels of being and development through philosophy, particularly through the resolution of the opposites. I will also consider the nature of soul's luciform body and its relationship to world soul. I include several direct quotes in the following pages from scholars to support my position. Being a psychologist and not a philosopher, I make generous use of others' work.

The Structure of the Soul

In *Reading Ancient Texts, Presocratics and Plato* (Suzanne Stern-Gillet and Kevin Corrigan, 2008) we find:

The Platonic Dialogues, generally speaking, present us with many different perspectives on the soul, and it is important at the outset to emphasize the complexity of the picture. The dialogues depictions of the structure of soul ranges from a simple, incomposite soul in the Phaedo and Republic 10 to a tripartite structure in Republic 4 and the Phaedrus (where soul is simultaneously both human and divine) and then to a bipartite structure (immortal/mortal) in the Timaeus and also in the Laws. (p. 102)

I will describe the tripartite and bipartite structures of soul later because I want to start with Ellen Wagner's (2001, 11-12) important conclusion that "several scholars (Archer-Hind, Crombie, Guthrie, Cornford, Grube, Taylor) all describe the three parts of the tripartite soul as divisions that can be reconciled with the simple soul of the *Phaedo*, being functions and forces that still belong to the unity of a "single soul." Uniting these divisions elevates the soul and constitutes its progress. "The soul's progress toward the Forms is the result of resolution of conflict among its three components" (p. 11). The nature of soul's progress, which is resolving conflicts and oppositions through philosophy, transforms soul's orientation from identification with the mortal and sensible realm to the immortal.

In this same vein, another view reconciles the perspective of the simple soul found in the *Phaedo* and the tripartite divisions:

The Republic theory involves not so much a division of soul as an integration into soul of mental or psychological functions that had been assigned, somewhat problematically to the body…what the Republic offers is a theory of soul which, among other things, allows attribution of (in principle) all mental or psychological functions to a single subject, the soul. Moreover, the Republic theory also offers an attractive and well supported articulation of desire into different kinds, which has profound implications both for what it is to have a soul (or mind) in optimal condition and for how it is this condition is best brought about. (Lorenz 2009)

The conflicts inherent in the divisions of soul are fundamental to its eventual transformation and "optimal condition." Such a condition refers to re-collecting into soul what seems to belong to the body and resolving desire stemming from appetite and the spirited aspect, in order to raise awareness into a unified sphere.

As I have mentioned, Plato's soul is elaborated from a simple soul into a bipartite and tripartite structure. In *The Gorgias* (Plato 1996, vol. IV, 493), the soul is described as bipartite or having two distinct parts, a rational and non-rational aspect. The non-rational element, the passions and desires and impulses, are what keep a man immersed in the sensible world. This non-rational aspect, which is the soul's lower nature, has a worthwhile role in the life of the soul but only if the rational part is in control. The rational aspect is referred to as wisdom or intelligence and if it doesn't keep the non-rational in check, then the qualities acquired by the soul can become harmful. The qualities within the bipartite structure are neither advantageous nor harmful. They become so through the presence and influence of whichever side of the soul is active.

Each side of the bipartite soul has a guiding principle defining its action and motion. The irrational side has a natural compulsion to follow the desire for pleasure, the other side a slowly developed quality of being able to perceive what is most prudent, and then also to have developed the capacity to follow what has been discerned with the best action. What is best is not necessarily identical to what a person wants. Soul struggles, first following one, and then the other. Persistent rational mastery is called temperance, a goal of the philosophic life that does not imply what we usually think of as rationality. The rational nature refers to a level of being and it has the capacity to be present to higher being. Temperance generates harmony in its wake, which is an energizing quality the soul then possesses (Plato 1996, vol. IV, 317). The energy of harmony is produced through its organizing and teleological influence; it leads a soul forward. When the irrational is superior, it disharmonizes the rational part. In this case, harmony becomes a latent energetic feature. The soul cannot adequately realize all its functions and capabilities unless the irrational is prescribed and regulated by rational insight.

In the *Republic*, *Timaeus*, and *Phaedrus*, the soul is described as tripartite. These three different parts are the rational, spirited, and appetitive. Each desires different experiences. The appetites crave bodily pleasures, the spirited seeks art and science, and the rational seeks contemplation of the Forms. The rational or intellective soul is the goal. It is the basis of the luciform body, which connects the individual soul to world soul. The intellective soul originates in the intelligible sphere and is immortal. The other two parts are added because they are necessary to our mortal lives and therefore our lower, sensible nature.

In an advance from the discussion of soul in the *Phaedo*, where conflict exists only between itself and the body, in the *Republic* Book 10, Plato admits of conflict within the parts of the soul itself. Harmony occurs when spirit and appetite submit to reason because each part of soul then achieves the best and truest pleasure natural to it. Each dimension is rightfully responsible for doing its own work. Knowing oneself and caring for the soul implies directing "each to its own" with the result being an order and beauty within, or a harmonizing of the three principles of the soul. Plato discusses it as the intervals of three terms, the lowest, highest, and the mean, linking together and making a unit. In this act there is "one man instead of many [a person who is] self-controlled and in unison…" (1961, 686).

The internal conflict posed by the "many" within, is the material with which soul organizes and reorganizes its experience and priorities. Impulses from the two lower parts cause craving; the appetites crave bodily experience, possession, and profit. The spirited aspect craves mastery, conquest, ambition, reputation, status, and honor. The rational aspect craves learning (Rowe 1984, 103). The spirited part generates emotion, like anger. The appetites generate lower desires of all kinds. Passions and emotions are promoted to true psychic activities in the *Republic,* and when they are in order, the intellective and spirited aspects control appetite. For example, the rational is in control when a person can resist gratification of an appetite that reason rejects. The soul's apparent fragmentation into parts is due to association with the body and the irrational nature, which is associated with the sensible man. The two lower elements of the tripartite soul, the appetite and spirited, are inoperative when soul is discarnate.

The three parts of soul have their seat in the brain, the solar plexus or chest area, and the belly. The immortal intellective part is placed in the head because as *Timaeus* says, this part of the body is "a most divine member, and the sovereign ruler of our whole corporeal composition" (Plato 1996, vol. II, 446). The spirited is in the solar plexus and the appetitive is in the belly. Each principle represents a different level of mental development rather than being a completely separate feature (Taylor 1960, 83). Soul, as a real, subtle, luciform substance of being, involves development, evolution, and change. Through becoming, it transforms according to the motions within it. These motions are constant and involve the three energies of appetite, spirit, and intellect:

> It [soul] either converts itself to things subordinate, and acquires a knowledge of sensibles; or it converts itself to itself, and sees all things in itself because it is an omniform image containing the reasons of all things; or it extends itself to the intelligible, and beholds ideas. (Plato 1996, vol. IV, 306)

Experience leads to insight about whether intellective, spirited, or appetitive aspects are in charge of perception, apprehension, and act. Finding the appropriate balance of these elements is a process of acquiring virtue. In the philosophical life, the philosopher attains to the highest degree of virtue, creating a quality of subtlety in soul that liberates from the passions and delivers all the lower energies into their highest purpose: contemplating the immortal Form and the One. Soul has reached the realization of its own potential at this stage of development.

The Immortality of the Soul

The immortality of the soul was a great concern to Plato, and several arguments were developed to establish this in different dialogues, each having a degree of effectiveness. In the *Phaedo*, the Cyclical Argument is "generally not taken as a serious attempt … rather as an initial effort intended to be supplemented" (Wagner 2001, 13), but three other arguments in this dialogue are more successful. The recollection argument declares that since we know things that cannot be known by sense, our souls must have acquired knowledge before birth, and we recollect this knowledge in life by contact with the Forms. The affinity argument, which is considered famous but flawed, posits the soul's similarity to the Form, and thus its resemblance to the divine, while the body resembles what is mortal. The final argument states that the soul is alive so will never admit of death, but will instead leave the body (14).

A few more words on the Affinity Argument from Lorenz (2009) in "Ancient Theories of Soul," because he brings out material concerning the nature of soul's disposition, as well as its immortality:

Although Greeks at the time of Plato did not generally believe in the immortality of the soul, Socrates and Plato asserted its existence after death. Socrates says not only that the soul is immortal but that it also contemplates truth after its separation from the body at the time of death … [the] argument sheds light on the nature of the soul's dispersion after death—-distinguishes two kinds of things—-perceptible, composed of parts, subject to dissolution and destruction and things that are not perceptible but intelligible (grasped by thought) not composed of parts and exempt from dissolution and destruction. The argument leaves room for the idea that souls are not forms but are nevertheless intelligible, partless and imperishable. Body and soul differ in kind. One being perishable, etc—-the other not … soul is most like and most akin to intelligible being and body is most like the perishable and perceptible being.

This commentary supports the idea that what is not united in the soul, those elements that are in parts and therefore perceptible by outer sense, are perishable. That which has been united and therefore not made of parts, or no longer made of parts, is eternal and of the intelligible realm, although not a Form. This commentator goes on to say that:

The argument leaves it open whether soul is a perfectly respectable member of intelligible reality, the way human bodies are perfectly respectable members of perceptible reality, or whether, alternatively, soul has some intermediate status in between intelligible and perceptible being, rising above the latter but merely approximate to the former.

The body is a member of the perceptible world as is concrete or sensible reality. The soul resides beyond sense, in the intelligible realm. Soul's proximate location to the Form, suggested in this passage to be in an intermediate status between the Forms and sensible reality, or on the level of Form, is an important feature that reappears in Jung, which I will discuss at length later.

To conclude with the arguments for immortality, in the *Phaedrus* the soul is said to be immortal because it is self-moving (Wagner 2001, 14), and in the *Timaeus* it is said that the soul's immortal part is reason, while its two lower parts are constructed from matter, of which the body is made. The two lower parts do not survive bodily death but the immortal part returns to the star from which it originates (p. 14).

Establishing the immortality of Plato's soul is important as it is central to the goals of philosophy. These goals are to transform the part to the whole and consciousness of sensible reality to consciousness in soul, in order to return to the pure being of the One, which is our immortal home. In Plato the soul descends in order to transcend its abode in the sensible world by becoming conscious of the forms and the One above. Seven different aspects of the soul are identified in the *Phaedo* that signify its capacity to develop consciousness of the form and its immortality. Soul is understood

> as the element in us that must be cared for if we are to have genuine well being; … as the "true self;" … as intellect or reason, that which apprehends the Forms in a kind of intellectual "vision;" … as the rational self in opposition to emotion and appetite; … as the subject of general conscious states; … in the traditional sense as a life principle; and … taken in general to mean a sort of "soul-stuff." (Wagner 2001, 5)

Soul in the Third

The care of the soul brings about the "true self," that which can apprehend the Forms and the One. The reconciliation of the opposites, for example the mortal and immortal aspects, and the appetites and the reason, occur in the soul because it exists between the higher and lower levels of being, between sense and Form, in a third ontological category that is of the eternal, intelligible world. Plato (1996, vol. II, 435) describes the creation of this third ontological category when he says, "From an essence impartible, and always subsisting according to sameness of being, and from a nature divisible about bodies, he mingled from both a third form of essence, having a middle subsistence between the two." Being in the middle, soul in the third unites the different realms of being and becoming, the intelligible and sensible.

Thomas Taylor (1758-1835) (1996, vol. II, 435) translated Plato's *Dialogues* a few centuries ago. In his translation of the *Timaeus*, Plato's soul is created in the third, commingled with the principles of sameness and difference. These three forces, essence, sameness, and difference, are the foundation for soul's structure and infinite radius throughout the universe. The significance of the nature of "same" and "different" in soul is that "same" reflects unity in the world of Forms and "different" reflects the parts of the lower world of particulars in sense. In Hamilton and Cairns (1961, 1163) edited version of the *Dialogues* the *Timaeus* is translated by Benjamin Jowett. In this text, Plato refers to soul's existence in the third between the intelligible realm of Form and the sensible body when he remarks that God "put intelligence in soul, and soul in body … the world came into being—a living creature truly endowed with soul and intelligence."

To Plato the universe and the human being, the macro-cosmos and microcosmos, are identified as having a center or midpoint of soul where the Form can be reflected in order to enliven the body. The relationship between soul and intellect is inherent although effort is required to make this conscious. Soul at the midpoint unifies the whole: "Two things cannot be rightly put together without a third; there must be some bond of union between them. And the fairest bond is that which makes the most complete fusion of itself and the things which it combines" (1961, 1163). Soul's unity or sameness with both the higher and lower worlds is described further on in the same translation.

From the being which is indivisible and unchangeable, and from that kind of being which is distributed among bodies, he com-pounded a third and intermediate kind of being. He did likewise with the same and different, blending together the indivisible kind of each with that which is portioned out in bodies. Then taking the three new elements, he mingled them all into one form …. When he had mingled them with the intermediate kind of being and out of three made one, he again divided this whole … each portion being a compound of the same, the different, and being. (p. 1165)

This discussion proceeds to detail the number of intervals included in creation, all of which are imbued with soul and its three elements of being, sameness, and difference, and are "bent into a circular form" (1961, 1166). This circle is made to move in a uniform revolution with the motion of the same in the outer circle and the motion of the difference in the inner circle. When God brought the entire universe together with the soul, "he united them center to center. The soul, interfused everywhere from the center to the circumference of heaven, of which also she is the external envelopment … began a divine beginning of never-ceasing and rational life" (p. 1166).

In this circular arrangement, the divine intelligible realm is indivisible, unchangeable and the same, and the sensible world is divided, changeable, different, and distributed among bodies. In between these two, the third or intermediate kind of being holds the circling levels of the worlds together. In the macrocosmic universe and the microcosmic human, the intermediate being between the Forms and sensible reality is soul, who through its sameness can unite with the unchangeable world of Forms and through its difference, the changing, divided, differentness of the sensible realm.

Experience in life is determined by soul's orientation. Plato goes on to explain:

The soul is invisible and partakes of reason and harmony, and, being made by the best of intellectual and everlasting natures, is the best of things created. And because she is composed of the same and of the different and of being these three, and is divided and united in due proportion, and in her revolutions returns upon herself, the soul, when touching anything which has being, whether dispersed in parts or undivided, is stirred through all her powers to declare the sameness or difference of that thing and some other, and to what individuals are related, and by what affected, and in what way and how and when, both in the world of generation and in the world of immutable being. And when reason, which works with equal truth, whether she be in the circle of the diverse or of the same— in voiceless silence holding her onward course in the sphere of the self-moved—when reason, I say, is hovering around the sensible world and when the circle of the diverse also moving truly imparts the intimations of sense to the whole soul, then arise opinions and beliefs sure and certain. But when reason is concerned with the rational, and the circle of the same moving smoothly declares it, then intelligence and knowledge are necessarily achieved. And if anyone affirms that in which these two are found to be other than the soul, he will say the very opposite of the truth. (1961, 1166-1167)

Soul's capacity to mirror intelligence and knowledge or sense-based opinion and belief is reflected in a more modern commentary on Plato's soul, "Essays on Plato's Psychology" (Wagner, 2001, 3). Ellen Wagner states in her introduction that Plato's soul "bridges the gap between the sensible world and the realm of Forms, making knowledge possible as well as explaining the nature of moral character, its perfecting and its degeneration." In another paragraph she states that Plato's soul "occupies an uneasy hybrid position between Forms and sensibles, being invisible and perhaps noncomposite yet subject at times to the kind of instability from which sensibles invariably suffer" (p. 7). Plato's soul "has features of both sensibles and forms depending on its cognitive and perceptual activities" (p. 7). The human soul can either ascend by developing consciousness of higher being or fall into the lower sphere by identifying with the sensible sphere.

The Dual-Unity of Soul in the Third

This hybrid nature of the self in soul is based on Plato's philosophy of the same and the different existing with the being of soul. Soul's capacity to "be" in unity and "be" in difference, aware of only the differences or aware of the difference in unity, allows a person the freedom to choose its own destiny. Soul, depending on its activity, can look downward into the sensible realm and become attached and enamored with its sameness with the lower realm. Or soul can look upward and gaze at the intelligible sphere of Form and the One and become immersed in and identified with its sameness with the higher world. The process of growth is a constant tension of developing and holding conscious degrees of sameness yet difference between the two.

Dual-unity has the crucial function of holding the worlds together, as well as the inner world of humankind. At all times, the unity of soul with Form and archetype and therefore the One or Self keeps all the parts or dualities of ego and sense together, first outside of consciousness and also when a person wakes up to the nature of the self. The journey of growth and healing in both Plato and Jung is an incremental gathering together of the parts, differences or dualities into the unity of consciousness. Importantly, soul's dual-unity is what allows human beings freedom or free will. A person always uses free will when deciding to invest in certain values or experiences and it is only through using the freedom allotted to us that we can discover the macro-cosmos, or what appears externally as the universe, in the soul.

The parts or levels of the macro-cosmos slowly come into consciousness in a unity as the parts of the psyche knit together. Because the psyche mirrors the macrocosm, the totality of worlds can be actualized through dual-unity in the midpoint of soul. When the lower world of sense and ego and its corresponding cosmos, physical earth, are held in consciousness with the immaterial, spiritual world, the two opposites remain a two but become a one in experience on the higher level of soul. The two plus one is the third or soul, which holds the all. Spanning the cosmos, the conscious individual soul lives here on earth while immersed to some degree in experiences of the divine above. Let's go on and examine how this process of development occurs through philosophy.

Soul's Development through Philosophy

Acquiring Virtue

Finding the balance in the third or soul through philosophy is a process of acquiring virtue, moral values that pertain to the spiritual life and lead to actualization of that life. In order to reach such an actualization, a person must learn to contemplate the Forms and the One in a process of higher cognitive growth that combines being and knowledge, rather than engaging in a purely emotional process, for example the ecstasy of initiation in the mystery religions (Kraut 1992, 232). Experiencing the Forms is cognitive because it means acquiring knowledge of divine objects, which makes the soul more identical to those objects. In this way, the soul receives its salvation through philosophy. Salvation refers to the birth of wisdom, and wisdom brings together the links in Plato among soul, salvation, and knowledge. Since learning in philosophy is also an experience of being it will "lead back souls to that end from which as a principle they made their first descent" (Plato 1996, vol. IV, 312). Transformation in the self through acquiring virtue brings a soul home to its origin in the divine One.

The salvation of the soul is epistemological and ontological because of the relationship between body and soul. The body cannot exist by itself, it depends on soul for its being (onto) and its knowledge (episteme). Plato writes: "The Demiurge 'made soul prior to [the] body and [it is] older than it in origin and excellence, to be the body's mistress and governor'" (Robinson 1970, 69). Soul, in turn, receives its knowledge from the Forms and the One above, and although soul is not a Form, it exists in the intelligible sphere and its life comes from the One above.

Soul was given ontological priority over body in the cosmology because it came into being as it's ordering principle. The soul, it is said in *Laws*, Book 10 (Plato, trans. 1961, 1447), was "Not fire, nor air, but soul which was there to begin with—it will be perfectly true to say that it is the existence of soul which is most eminently natural." As cause, soul is good, communicates life, and moves all in the direction of good. Body, as image of the invisible soul, is unintelligent, subject, and no cause of its own except movement away from the good, which is contrary to the natural condition.

The soul, although an ordering principle, is not strictly identified with the world of Forms. As mentioned earlier, it is described like a Form, indestructible and ungenerated, unique and eternal. Plato says in the *Phaedo* (Plato, trans.1996, vol. 4, 258) that the human soul is "most *similar* [italics added] to the divine, immortal, intelligible, uniform and indissoluble nature, and which always subsists similarly according to the same." Having the same qualities as a form, it is different. The Form remains in the intelligible realm when it makes its imprint in the receptacle, which is only a Form copy or image. Conversely, the soul comes to abide in the receptacle in a body that is "human, mortal, void of intellect, multiform, dissoluble, and which never subsists according to the same" (p. 258).

Soul descends from intelligible being and while embodied in the sensible world encompasses both being and becoming. Although "true reality," the soul must work to realize its own being and become conscious of its "likeness" to the divine life above. It is soul alone that is able to change its state of experience and presence over a wide spectrum of conditions, from the lowest level of illusion or opinion in the sensible world, to the highest state of presence to the One. The state of the soul changes or transforms upwards through acquiring knowledge.

In the earlier discussion on cosmology, I established that the receptacle receives the image of the form copy in the sensible world and gives it body, making it like itself. This state of receiving the image as sense is the first level of knowledge. It is referred to as "illusion," in the divided line allegory mentioned earlier because it is furthest down epistemologically and ontologically, remote from true being and subject to the swiftly changing conditions of sense, space and time, and the chaotic world of necessity. The act of creation that put reason over necessity brings chaos into a direction towards the good. This inborn order where reason can potentially rule over necessity is also given to the soul who comes to life in the sensible realm. Developing the inborn reason (called the rational element in the bipartite and tripartite definitions) leads to the growth of philosophical virtues in the soul.

The growth of virtue in the soul is incremental but eventually contains and organizes the chaos of necessity. Beginning its philosophical sojourn in illusion, perceiving Form copies in the receptacle of physical nature and asleep to inner being, the soul is in proximity to the darkness of non-being or becoming. The culmination of soul's journey is unity with the intelligible Forms, aware of the light of the One. The soul, if developed through philosophy, not only leads a life of harmony but is also prepared for death, according to Socrates in the *Phaedo*. If one has developed the soul by transforming it with the virtues, then it has reached a degree of mastery over the body. The appetitive and spirited dimensions of the lower nature that are under the power of the body and its senses involving pleasure, pain, and emotional attachments to worldly objects and aims are enjoyed but not overvalued. Mastery introduces steadiness, coherence, and freedom from the many influences affecting the body. Such a state is called wisdom, and it achieves liberation from necessity and its receptacle, within itself and in the world.

At death, the soul that has identified with the virtues in philosophy and attained the higher states of knowledge called *dianosis* and *noesis* in the divided line allegory is present to and unified with the forms. Therefore, it has the substance or being of the intelligible forms along with experience of the divine One. In Plato, one acquires knowledge through presence in being, or higher being. Presence is identifying with or mirroring the higher dimension through its unity or sameness with the higher Form, thereby sharing substance or being with the Forms and the divine One while remaining separate. The dual-unity of presence is achieved through mastery of the lower nature and sensible reality and signifies freedom. Socrates, in Plato (1961, 46), when preparing for his death, was explaining to his friends that he expected to join very good men and divine masters when he left the body. He expected this post-mortem life because through philosophy, he had achieved a steadiness of presence to the higher level of being, called wisdom. The soul that does not achieve this level of presence or knowledge does not have the same destiny.

The destiny of a soul who has not achieved philosophy or a life of virtue is still grappling with the irrational, lower nature. Known as a "bad" man in the *Phaedo*, his destiny may include transmigration into an animal because of a lifetime of cultivating personal attributes and qualities that mirror the level of being of an animal. This attitude about animals being less important or valuable then humans no longer applies to a contemporary liberal sensibility, but he was using the metaphor of animal nature to indicate an undeveloped state of human being. The habits and the relationships such men have create states of evil in the body, so these qualities exist after death in beastly form (or I might add, in a mind of beastly form). On the other hand, decent citizens become humans again of the same kind they were previously, or they transmigrate into communities that are representative of such cooperation, like bees or ants. Those who have grown beyond the collective into individual soul are called the wise and go to the divine Gods in their next life.

Battling Vice

The role of vice and ignorance in a person's soul are seen as disease and deformity, which is what creates the "bad" in humans. Plato felt that virtue was the only path that protected the soul against the "bad" taking hold of a man and furthermore that it was a constant struggle to avoid the bad and become good. As soul learns to realize the good, or the life of forms and the One, it must transmigrate or pass in and out of physical life again and again. Every time the soul cycles through life in the physical body it manifests as the being it is. In other words, it lives according to the being and substance it has awakened within, while previously sojourning in the sensible world. When the soul returns to sensible reality it embodies that spectrum of perception, apprehension, and under-standing or knowledge commensurate with its own state.

The incarnation of soul and its reason over sense and its receptacle always assures that the forces of necessity will eventually be a guiding factor towards return to the One. However, the soul, when controlled more by necessity than its own intelligible being, is under the sway of chance or fate since necessity is impersonal. Driven by fate, life events are experienced according to random desire and are perhaps disorgan-ized, chaotic, and even destructive. When the works of reason (virtue) and the intelligible sphere direct life through the soul, events occur according to providence. Providence is the expression of divine purpose. A life centered in or close to the intelligible realm of Form, and, thus, the One, progresses with an intrinsic pattern intuitive to the individual. Such a life expresses the order of the soul.

A life organized by providence is orchestrated through the work of philosophy. The principle of the philosophic life, "Know thyself," is expressed over the lintel of the Delphic Temple in Greece. Acquiring this knowledge is the birth of the soul in awareness and the birth of wisdom in thought. According to Plato, Socrates saw himself as the "midwife of the soul" in that his aim was bringing young men to thoughts of wisdom rather than illusion. Plato took this mission up himself. To conceive of one's own soul is to be conscious beyond the attributes of life expressed through the physical body. In Plato's dialogue, Socrates believed that few achieved this awareness and he expressed it to Theaetetus in his remark, "there are some...whose minds, as I judge, have never conceived at all" (Plato 1961, 856). He refers to those who have failed to grasp the procreant nature of the soul.

These people never come to life. Instead they remain dead, entombed within the body and asleep to higher realities and their own divine nature.

The philosophic life aims at the care of the soul so that it may reach its zenith of development. Thomas Taylor (Plato 1996, 258) remarks in his notes that "the soul rules over the body. For that which uses an instrument possesses dominion over it [13.20]." The body is the soul's instrument, and the developed soul relates to the body as a cherished instrument, caring for, ruling, and deliberating over its own lower nature in order to lead it to its birth in wisdom; this is ultimate well-being. The whole person is healed in this process, not just a part. Unlike us, the Greeks would not attempt to heal only a part of a person, like a limb, or a diseased organ. The birth of the soul or wisdom in thought affects harmony in the body, mind, and spirit. It creates unity, instills order into disorder, the rational into the irrational, and the divine into the material experience of a person. This ordering is the healing of body and soul through the spiritual science of virtue.

The philosophic life of virtue strives to separate the visible, sensible body and the invisible, subtle soul. The awareness of the separation of these opposites allows for a conscious integration of these same opposites, resulting in the transformation of the embodied soul from a concrete perception and experience to an understanding of invisible intelligibles. This higher being reflects a conscious unity of sense with the intelligible forms, an awareness that transcends the previous level of consciousness, which was awake to sense and asleep to soul. This transformation was pursued in Orphism (one of the mystery cults active in Plato's era). Both philosophy and Orphism involved purification as a method of practice, such as vegetarianism. Efforts to achieve purity continued on the mental and emotional level as well, through the use of intellect and reason culminating in the soul's liberation.

Transmigration after death into another human body instead of subtle angelic existence reflected incomplete purification, or the influence of impulse over reason in the soul. Human souls must master the impulsive, irrational element of the soul that dominates their physical existence. In Book 10 of *The Laws* (Plato 1961), the soul's life is described as a process of purification and assimilation to the divine. Because the soul is the source of changes and rearrangements experienced in life, it is responsible for those things good and bad, beautiful and ugly, just and unjust. Learning to sort out pleasure and pain from the rational nature is exchanging them, not one for the other, but each one in turn for wisdom or true virtue, for example courage, temperance, and justice. Those who live the philosophical life are able in death to "return and dwell in his native star" (p. 1171). In Taylor's translation (Plato 1996, vol. IV, 295n), Plato says the philosophic soul returns after death "to the pure habitation on high, dwelling on the aetherial earth," translated by Olympiodorus, according to Taylor's commentary, as "in the heavens with luciform bodies."

By mastering the passions and lower nature through philosophy, a human being contributes its part to the whole of perfection:

The soul allows its circle of the Same to control by reason the irrational turmoil introduced into itself by earth, air, fire, and water. …Only then will the soul 'return once more to the form of its first and best condition…the optimum *human* condition, where one's rational activity and control over one's lower soul is the microcosmic counterpart of the eternally rational activity of World Soul. (Robinson 1970, 88-89).

The passions and appetite are the irrational aspect of the human soul. One needs to master them in order to escape the tendency to be drawn into the sense world again after death. Made in the image of the rational, the irrational lower nature is subtle but also corporeal, "this nature also is corporeal, consisting of a corporeal life, and a certain body more attenuated than this visible body" (Plato 1996, vol.IV, 316).

They proceeded to fashion . . . a soul of another nature which was mortal, subject to terrible and irresistible affections—first of all, pleasure, the greatest incitement to evil; then, pain, which deters from the good; also rashness and fear, two foolish counselors, anger hard to be appeased, and hope easily led astray—these they mingled with irrational sense… (Plato 1961, 1193)

The irrational element of the soul identifies with the physical body because of the unity or sameness aspect of the dual-unity that organizes soul. Souls that remain the same as, or bound to the visible nature through the irrational element remain heavy through sympathy and sink down ontologically.

Ultimately, in order for the soul to consciously return to its immortal home in the intelligible divine it must do battle with the irrational. Experienced as a myriad of opposites involving pleasure and pain, the irrational is stirred in the soul but experienced in the physical. The worst evil is, "That the soul of every man is compelled, through experiencing some extreme pleasure or pain, to imagine that whatever most strongly arouses such feelings is most vivid and real—although, of course, it is not…" (Bluck 1955, 83).

All pleasure and pain have a profound influence on character and therefore on destiny. "As if armed with a nail, [pleasure and pain] fasten and rivet the soul to the body, cause it to become corporeal, and fill it with an opinion, whatever the body asserts is true" (Plato 1996, vol. IV, 262). Without mastering the irrational, the soul at death "swiftly falls again into another body, and, becoming as it were sown, is engendered…destitute of a divine, pure, and uniform association" (pp. 262-263). The soul in this circumstance is caught on the wheel of reincarnation and must continue its immortal work of turning towards what is best.

The development of virtue (*arête*) is the development of moral excellence. As life's highest purpose, virtue blends Platonic knowledge and being into one principle. In *The Gorgias*, the discussion between

Socrates, Polus and then Callicles about virtue and the nature of pleasure and the good concludes with Plato's Socrates pointing out that knowledge is a necessary but not sufficient condition for virtue, because self-mastery must also play its part. *Sophrosyne* is a quality of character often rendered as "temperance" that consists of the control over the irrational desires. According to Rowe, the orderly soul 'must also possess the other virtues" (Rowe 1984, 98).

Knowledge that is being implies that mind or soul inevitably imitates the character of what it habitually contemplates. The mind knows of, knows how, and knows by acquaintance (Robinson 1970, 4). Knowing "of" something is naming what it is in the concrete sensible world. Knowing "how" is about its cause in the abstract sense. Knowing through "acquaintance" is knowledge through presence, participation in the real life of the divine Forms. Presential knowledge is linked with high moral character. It is coeval with contemplation of the forms of virtue.

In *Laws*, Book 12 (Plato 1961, 1507) virtue is said to have four parts. The "chief of them all is understanding, and it should be the aim of the other three parts." Full virtue is the attainment of the single virtues. Each is a separate reality different from the others. "Wisdom, temperance, courage, justice, and holiness…are parts [of virtue], but like the parts of a face, resembling neither the whole nor each other and each having a separate function" (p. 341). All characteristics of virtue are produced by the soul gazing upward toward the intelligible spheres.

The vices of intemperance, injustice, ignorance, fear, and impiety are from gazing downward into the lower sensible spheres. By contemplating the intelligible, soul is purified of vice like the body must be relieved of disease.

> There are two kinds of evil in the soul—the one which is generally called vice… the other which they call ignorance … cowardice,

intemperance, and injustice are all alike forms of disease in the soul, and ignorance, of which there are all sorts of varieties, to be deformity. (Plato 1961, 971).

Plato's Cave Allegory

The condition of the soul is therefore advanced through knowledge, which relieves it of its deformity. "The soul acquires knowledge and is kept going and improved by learning and practice…by inactivity, dullness, and neglect of exercise, it learns nothing and forgets what it has learned" (Plato 1961, 858). This progress of the soul's development through knowledge and its corresponding level of being are illustrated by Plato's cave allegory. The story is about the soul's development through realizing ever-increasing levels of knowledge and being, or light. From illusion to wisdom and virtue, all the levels are achieved in the soul. The process is expressed through the metaphor of a pilgrimage out of a cave-like prison, which represents a soul hemmed in by darkness, vice, and ignorance of true reality or being.

The progress into virtue and out of the cave takes place in four stages. The first stage is where most spend their lives, seeing only shadows and hearing only echoes. Perceiving shadows and echoes means the self-preoccupation of observing only the basest representations of reality, those shaped by pleasure and pain in the body. At this stage the soul exists latent in the sensible world and there is no consciousness of the intelligible world in life or after death. Instead, consciousness reflects the illusion of random images of fantasy, moving according to unrestrained desires. In death, consciousness continues to reflect the images that contributed to its external orientation in life.

The second stage is the ability to look at the actual objects casting the shadows, which are images that are Form copies. The soul perceiving the form copy has opinions about the objects and the actions of the sensible world. The opinions are independent from pleasure or pain but are still derived through physical experience. This orientation never admits knowledge or true virtue. Because consciousness constantly shifts according to the environment and senses, there is no permanent substance mirrored in the soul. Therefore, little permanent character carries over to "remember" or recollect (an act of knowledge in Plato) during the next cycle of transmigration.

The third stage is the capacity to think or contemplate the divine forms, but only in an uncoordinated plurality. This is the ability to perceive reality in the mental sphere but not yet the unity of first principles. Consciousness is realized in soul at this stage because attention shifts inward, and internal concentration and apprehension organize the meaning of experience more than external stimulation. When internal concentration is steady and concentrated, virtue can be sustained and wisdom and understanding can be experienced in the intelligible sphere. This brings substance and order to soul making it an organ of perception. Reflection assists the soul in returning to virtue when it "falls" into lower states, becoming more disorganized and reactive to external events.

The fourth stage is actual contemplation of the One, or the first principle of reality (Raven 1965, 172-173). This happens in degrees according to how consistently one can stay with this level of contemplation. Glimpses that grow to a more constant state reflect the soul's destination in the sojourn of return: the full realization of soul and its subtle, light body that is an organ of being and knowledge, in company with divine being.

The soul cannot be dragged too quickly out of the cave and into the upper world of true reality, for its eyes would be blinded by radiance and its experience would be one of suffering. Taking steps out of the cave is like moving up the rungs of a ladder (Raven 1965, 116). It is Eros, or love, that first drives a person to search for the first rung of ascension. This first rung is in the image of what is like him, or "his like." One's like is a representation of a level of Good and can be the good of the appetitive, spirited, or intellective parts of the soul.

On the first rung of the ladder, one's like involves the love of sensible reality and the physical world. Acquiring virtue on that level is practical virtue, and then one moves to the spirited and beyond to the rung of the intellective. Each level in the ascent embraces all the earlier levels. As the earlier rungs come under the control of the rational, called self-control, we are able to truly enjoy the pleasures of our lower impulses because soul has become balanced and integrated. Each part is in order according to its own nature.

Failing to strike out on the pilgrimage from the cave is a failure to nurture and care for the soul. Plato sees this as marking the soul with evil, produced by neglect.

> The marks branded on the soul by every evil deed—and that everything is crooked through falsehood and imposture, and nothing is straight because it has been reared a stranger to the truth….owing to the license and luxury and presumption and incontinence of its actions the soul is surcharged with disproportion and ugliness…" (Plato 1961, 305)

However, Plato believes no one is willingly bad.

> For no man is voluntarily bad, but the bad become bad by reason of an ill disposition of the body and bad education—things which are hateful to every man and happen to him against his will… Further, when to this evil constitution of body evil forms of government are added and evil discourses are uttered in private as well as in public, and no sort of instruction is given in youth to cure these evils, then all of us who are bad become bad from two causes which are entirely beyond our control. In such cases the planters are to blame rather than the plants, the educators rather than the educated. (Plato 1961, 1206-1207)

Even though it may not be one's will to lack virtue and therefore pursue evil ends, the consequences translate irreparably into fate.

If the soul is immortal we need to care for it, not only for the sake of …life, but also for the sake of all time…if we neglect it, we shall be running a great risk. …the only thing a soul takes with it to the other world is its education and culture which are said to be the greatest help or the greatest hindrance that the dead man can have…" (Bluck 1955, 128).

When the soul separates its intelligible life from the vessel of the body, it will return to its proper place, that which mirrors the rung of virtue it has attained advancing on the path towards the One.

Moral Being

The ultimate postmortem liberation and therefore the complete realization of soul is an attainment that Plato identifies with full virtue, made up of specific moral characteristics. Moral being is achieved by learning how to cherish and love the body from the detached, yet nurturing attitude of a higher idea, the idea that body is the vehicle of soul. The body becomes a conduit or medium of desire rather than a source. Eating, drinking, the senses, and sexual satisfaction are performed and experienced fully but not taken as ends. By maintaining awareness of the invisible nature of soul while engaging in bodily experience, one avoids confusion and vacillation. One is not dragged into "all kinds of fantasy and nonsense" (Bluck 1955, 51). One is able to avoid speech that affects the soul with evil, "When we do not speak in a becoming manner…[we] affect our souls with a certain evil" (Plato 1996, vol. IV, 297).

Correcting attitude, mastering behavior, and refocusing attention in relation to the body, one begins the ascent to virtue in the philosophic life. This is the first step out of the cave. It corrects faulty attitudes towards the body and provides for our material well-being. The furthering of insight into moral values and the application of these upon conduct differentiates real virtue from the ordinary virtue practiced by the majority, who remain unfortunately at the stages of illusion and opinion.

Ordinary virtue is for appearance only, verbal or actual behavior that masks real intention of another kind. Empty of value for the philosopher, this kind of virtue belongs to the social world of impressions. The petty affairs of men on the political and social scale no longer engage those focused on real virtue because of the strife, envy, and hate that result from the wrongs done according to ambition and outer gain. In *Laws*, Book 6, Plato reflects that men who are not intentionally taught real virtue, can be "more savage than anything on the face of the earth" (Plato 1961, 1344).

Development of soul is a movement from outer strife to inner conflict, then virtue. The apprehension of the One at the level of virtue is like "a blaze kindled by a leaping spark, it is generated in the soul and at once becomes self-sustaining" (Plato 1961, 1589). The spark that ignites into blaze is the soul mastering the oppositions of its lower nature. The soul fills with light from the divine forms above because attention has shifted from unity with the part below to unity with the whole above. Through this transformation in the dynamic of dual-unity one arrives at "'an innermost self within the human soul…wherein resides her virtue, which is wisdom' …that part of soul which resembles God" (Robinson 1970, 10-11).

Conflicts continue to demand attention to both ignite the blaze of light within soul and to keep it going. Each separate virtue in the whole of virtue causes distinct thoughts, feelings, and actions in the will of the person. When these conflicting pressures are reconciled between lower sense and higher spirit, they culminate in the character of a good man. That is, good in the sense of reflecting one's own soul, which reflects the intelligible sphere and the divine One. Plato reminds us of the limits imposed by necessity while embodied. Nothing can be constant, including goodness: "To be a good man—continuing good— is not possible, but a man may *become* good, and the same man bad…

" (Plato 1961, 338). Incessant effort is required for self-knowledge, virtue, and goodness. It is a constant process of education. The epitome of virtue is

> The wise or temperate man, and he only, will know himself, and be able to examine what he knows or does not know, and to see what others know and think that they know and do really know, and what they do not know and fancy that they know when they do not. No other person will be able to do this …. this is wisdom… for a man to know what he knows, and what he does not know. (Plato 1961, 112-113)

The wisdom of high moral character includes the capacity to recognize knowledge according to the being of each individual. Attaining wisdom is coeval with being aware in the third category and being able to return to it after getting captivated or lost in the sphere of the ego or sensible realm. This soul exists as a witness to any process or qualities it may experience. Affected but not lost in events that occur to the body, soul's reality in the eternal sphere has become a constant factor. It maintains a conscious dual-unity with both the lower and higher, enabling it to identify or be the same as the ego-laden world yet remain different. As well, soul remains identical with the intelligible sphere while remaining a different, a unique individual soul. Philosophy is a lifelong project, a lifestyle of developing consciousness. The student aims at contemplating the intelligible sphere unceasingly in order to remain in a state of unity.

World Soul and the Subtle Luciform Body

Presence to the higher world of intelligible form and the One is reflected in what Plato refers to as the "body" of the soul. Specifically, he connects an individual's realization of the highest virtue (wisdom) with the souls having become fully "real," which he equates with divine substance or body: "A soul in which justice and wisdom come to exist is real...something not visible has a body...the soul itself does possess a sort of body" (Plato 1961, 991).

Soul in the physical body of an individual related to the world of illusion and opinion only partakes of sensible reality and therefore has not become fully "real." However, its origin is in the eternal divine life given freely from the One, which exists in the intelligible seat of the soul. When soul joins with and awakens to its intelligible source, it becomes aware of its being, which is a substance. Soul's body is capable of receiving the substance associated with the higher realization of *dianoia* and *noesis*, the ultimate states of knowledge and being. The realness of the subtle body as compared to the realness of the physical body is a paradox in that "what is not, in some respect has being, and conversely that what is, in a way is not" (Plato 1961, 985).

The reality of the soul and its subtle body against the physical is emphasized in *The Sophist* when it is pointed out that the many images of physical reality can be seen by the physical eyes but not understood. Conversely, the subtle and invisible can be understood but not seen. "Seeing" the subtle body occurs not through the eyes but through the higher knowing of intuition derived from presence to the intelligible sphere of the forms and the One. Soul lives in a lower ontological category but carries the promise of development to the higher, from illusion to wisdom.

In each of its stages, from being in illusion (*eikasia*) to achieving its highest realization in a subtle body of wisdom (*noesis*), soul's power gives life and purpose to the physical body. The physical body always serves as a shell or tomb for the subtler soul living within it, whether one is aware of it or not.

The subtle body of soul is referred to in Plato as a "luciform body" (Plato 1996, vol. IV, 319) in his discussions of world soul, which he connects with the human soul. Luciform means light, therefore we can understand that the world's soul is made of light, a subtle, immaterial substance. World soul belongs to the earth, planets, and stars. It is descended from the intelligible world of forms and exists in the individual bodies of planets and stars as well as in a unity encompassing those. Having both a universal and individual role, world soul is the ground in which human soul exists: "in the formation of the immortal part of the human soul, [world soul]…is divided up into individual souls" (Robinson 1970, 87).

Placed initially by divine purpose in a star within world soul, each human soul descends into a sensible body as a latent power or being. The purpose of incarnating in a body is to become conscious of being a fully developed body of light, reunited with its star in world soul. World soul participates in and makes possible this realization of the individual soul by contributing light-substance to the individual soul, which becomes conscious by degree when the lower and higher parts of a person are integrated. When the lower is raised to the higher, it becomes that higher substance.

> When he (God) was framing the universe, he put intelligence in soul, and soul in body.…two things cannot be rightly put together without a third; there must be some bond of union with them. And the fairest bond is that which makes the most complete fusion of itself and the things which it combines…they will all of them of necessity become the same, and having come to be the same with one another will be all one. (Plato 1961, 1163)

When the individual soul unites its disparate parts, it becomes One with its highest sovereign part, and therefore realizes the luciform body of world soul with its center the divine One. Because world soul is in perfect unity with the intelligible sphere, the human soul who gains presence to world soul has knowledge of the beings of forms. The individual soul and world soul compose a differentiated pair that is also a unity, mirroring the dual-unity of soul and the intelligible sphere. It is the unity or linking among the levels of being that allows for subject and object to know each other. Such interpenetration of presence between worlds conducts divine life into the experience and knowledge of mortal life here on earth.

In Plato's *Epinomis* (1961, 1524-1525), world soul is given beauty and harmony in the life of the heavenly stars. Existing as living entities because they are endowed with the "fairest of bodies and the happiest and best of souls... [the stars are] imperishable, immortal, and divine... that which eternally does the same acts, in uniform way and for the same reasons... [they] accomplish their duty to all living creatures." The actions of world soul are movements, "the most glorious of dances" that precisely shape year, day and month—putting order into the universe" (p. 1525). The cosmic soul is a mind, and it is with this intelligence that the universe is ordered, given structure, takes action, and makes decisions, all resulting in its own pattern of organization.

The earth, like the stars, has a body and a soul that is mind. "The earth is a *pleroma* of the universe, it is a God. ...Hence, intellect and a rational soul must be suspended from it, and consequently it must have a luciform prior to this apparent body" (Plato 1996, vol. IV, 319). The luciform body supports the earthly, corporeal bulk. The physical body of the earth depends upon its soul, which is made prior to its earthly frame. The body and soul of the earth are united center-to-center and world soul is diffused throughout the entire body from center to circumference, including the heaven or intelligible sphere above the earth, the two being one. The never-ceasing rational life of world soul is invisible, partakes of reason and harmony, and is the "best of intellectual and everlasting natures" (Plato 1961, 1166).

Human soul has a luciform body as part of the luciform body of world soul because both are suspended from pure being. Plato refers to this in the *Republic* (trans. 1961, p. 576) as the universal Light, a supreme truth beyond all else that when realized in the soul of a statesmen, puts rational order or justice into political affairs.

The universal light descends into soul, but prior to that, it descends into a genus of daemons. A daemon is an angel, a being who is "immediately suspended…always perfect… and is immutable…but is not conjoined with the superessential…" (Plato 1996, vol. IV, 317-318). Different yet united to the divine universal light of the One, the daemon is in dual-unity with the intellect (forms), to the soul (rational), to nature (the physical), to the fifth level (corporeal-body), and the sixth (matter) (317-318). There is a daemon assigned to each individual embodied in the physical world. This daemon functions as a subtle influence guiding a person's actualization. The divine influence of the daemon is teleological, meaning that it is an inborn force that calls a person towards growth.

The light of the hierarchy of angels is equated with the sun, the symbol for the universal light. According to its realization in the soul, this light defines being. Less perfect than the light of the daemons, initially the soul's spark of light can only be reflected in images. When humans intentionally find the light within, divine life comes alive in understanding and in experience. It is the light of soul that perceives, grasps, then intuits and is present to a world. Without the light of the soul, the "eye" would remain dark.

In the *Timaeus,* the eye is inserted into the face in order to "minister in all things to the providence of the soul" (Plato 1961, 1173). The eye as part of the soul is made of a substance like fire that does not burn. It is a "pure fire which is within us" (p. 1173). This light or fire is made to flow through the eyes in a stream, and it can imbue images with numinous energy. This internal light coalesces with the light of day; the light from within meets the photons of light coming from external reality and "one body is formed…wherever light that falls from within meets with an external object. … causing the perception which we call sight" (p. 1174). The sense-based side of sight is informed by the light of the image within, which we discussed in the section on images and the intelligible sphere.

As the light of the eye, soul is "sunlike…[it] receive[s] the power which it possesses as an influx…dispensed from the sun…the offspring of the good" (Plato, 1961, 743). The light is a "third thing specifically and naturally adapted to this purpose … [without which]… vision will see nothing" (p. 743). The metaphor of the eye as light and therefore knowledge in the soul continues throughout the discussion:

> But when…they [the eyes] are directed upon objects illumined by the sun…fixed on the domain where truth and reality shine resplendent it apprehends and knows them…but when it inclines to that region which is mingled with darkness, the world of becoming and passing away, it opines only and its edge is blunted. (p. 743)

The eye is the proverbial window of the soul. When one's gaze (the eye) falls on the world of becoming or sensible reality, the light of the soul is blunted. When it beholds the higher realities it is illuminated.

Soul in Plato is a body of light that also has motion. In the *Phaedrus* (Plato 1961), movement is identified with soul because it is constantly transforming towards unity in the One. Since the external world is nonbeing and images that are form copies, it is the soul that moves external reality from within. Plato says that "a body deriving its motion from a source within itself is animate or *besouled*" (p. 493) and in "Laws X" the soul is said to be the universal cause of all change and motion" (p. 1451).

Self-motion is "the essence and definition of the soul" (Plato 1961, 493) and being cannot be bestowed fully in time. Therefore, Being emerges consecutively in the finite world of moving images. The circular movement around a center represents the souls motion, both individual and world. "As long as the heavens and the sun continue to move round, all things in heaven and earth are kept going whereas if all things were bound and brought to a stand all things would be destroyed" (Plato 1961, 858). The forms, the soul, and sensible man are all in motion. The One, who has no parts, "Does not change its place either by traveling anywhere and coming to be in something, or by revolving in the same place, or by changing (Plato 1961, 933). The One is immobile and bestows itself in the part that circles around and creates the motion appropriate to the dual-unity of being and becoming. Because the soul has the One at its center, it is the dual-unity of motion and stillness simultaneously.

The stillness of the One in the center of the soul emerges into movement in form and soul, but the outer image seen by sensible man is immobile. A different kind of immobility than the One at the center, the outer image has no life itself. It is en-souled from within. It is the soul that brings together the inner form and its copy within and in the outer world. The motion and light of the soul galvanize the image into constant change and motion, linking causality with external life through the forms.

Being and becoming as well as stillness and motion come together in the soul in the instant, the present moment. In *The Parmenides* the moment is described thus:

Passing between the two [past and future] … it will never overstep the present…if it is true of anything which is becoming that it can never pass beyond the present, it constantly stops becoming when it is at the present, and it then is whatever it may be that it was becoming. (p. 944)

The motion of the becoming soul is actual being in every present moment. This arrangement is what allows for the dual-unity of being and becoming to exist within the individual. Being, present in every moment of attention, flows into becoming on either side of the moment, in past and future. According to the condition of the soul, awareness is either plunged into the becoming world only, or grasps the dual-unities of being and becoming. It is soul whose motion bridges the dualism of the invisible and visible realities, the divine stillness of the One with the irrational forces of necessity involved in becoming. At its ultimate height, the soul steadily mirrors the light of the divine and being like it, reproduces the beauty and harmony of the cosmos.

Chapter Four
Jung's Soul

There is a strong resemblance in the way Plato and Jung conceived of the human soul. I make extensive use of Jung's own words because I want to bring out an obscure and perhaps controversial aspect of his work on the nature of the human psyche. Jung, like Plato, addressed the existence of soul in different stages, both in its undeveloped stage as a functional complex and in its more developed state as a non-ego complex entity in the third—a category of being between the Self and ego. I examine the particular ways Jung has addressed this non-ego complex orientated level of being he called the third and have found that his various assertions, when put together, define the individual soul distinct from the archetype, the Self, and the ego and its complexes.

I begin my discussion with a few words about the soul's immortality and follow with an exploration of the soul's structure, its dynamic of dual-unity, and the role of the transcendent function in soul's growth. In Jung, the role of the transcendent function is unique, and I will discuss it in several sections beginning on page 150. I conclude the discussion of soul with Jung's work on the psychoid, which is a scientific appraisal of the transcendent realm that Plato didn't need to explain, and Jung's consideration of the subtle body of soul. Plato described the immaterial, subtle body of soul as a luciform body or body made of light. Equivalent to the quantum nature of Jung's psychoid matter, light is therefore the basis of the subtle body in both.

Soul's Immortality

Jung's references to the immortality of the soul, eternity, and the transcendence of the human spirit exist throughout his *Collected Works*. These include his own declarations as well as statements made by others, such as philosophers (Nietzsche, Kant, and Schopenhauer), scientists (Kepler), alchemists (Hermes Trismegistus, Paracelsus, Goethe), and physicists (Pauli). In his work on Synchronicity and in chapters such as "Death and the Soul" in *The Structure and Dynamics of the Psyche*, he discusses the reality of a timeless, spaceless world whose existence he feels it is imperative to recognize culturally and individually, in order to augment the impoverished and even destructive one-sided attitude of the ego. In a long quote, Jung (1969c) explains how the evidence for parapsychological events such as telepathy points to immortality, or a life beyond time:

> The limitations of consciousness in space and time is such an overwhelming reality that every occasion when this fundamental truth is broken through must rank as an event of the highest theoretical significance, for it would prove that the space-time barrier can be annulled. The annulling factor would then be the psyche, since space-time would attach to it at most as a relative and conditioned quality. Under certain circumstances it could even break through the barriers of space and time precisely because of a quality essential to it, that is, its relatively trans-spatial and trans-temporal nature. This possible transcendence of space-time, for which it seems to me there is a good deal of evidence, is of such incalculable import that it should spur the spirit of research to the greatest effort. Our present development of consciousness is, however, so backward that in general we still lack the scientific and intellectual equipment for adequately evaluating the facts…the psyches's attachment to the brain, i.e., its space-time limitation, is no longer as self evident and incontrovertible as we have hitherto been led to believe. (p. 413)

Jung is convinced that the human psyche, and I will show in particular the human soul, exists in a transcendent sphere beyond time and space and is therefore exempt from death. Jung's whole project is about balancing what he calls the "exaggerated rationalization of consciousness" (1969c, 380) with a deeper appreciation of the many dimensions of the psyche. He hoped to do this by bringing an earlier clarity, understanding, and experience of the spirit into present-day knowledge, wishing for "harmony with the historical man … in such a way that the deeper chords in him are not drowned by the shrill strains of rationalism, and the precious light of individual consciousness is not extinguished in the infinite darknesses of the natural psyche" (p. 381). As we shall see, Jung's work on the transcendent function resolves the opposites of the rational and spiritual and elevates consciousness into the light of individual soul, which encompasses the shadow and the darkness of the natural psyche.

When Jung (1968a, 114) describes the transformation of consciousness through the transcendent function, he says it is "the transformation … of a corporeal into a spiritual being." The term spiritual implies immortal, supernatural, and incorporeal, and this transformation of the corporeal begins with soul located in the natural sphere and functional complex. Jung, like Plato, is concerned with instructing others how to develop their consciousness in order to encompass the macrocosm within the microcosm of soul, and thus realize its immortality. He says:

> If I recognize only naturalistic values, and explain everything in physical terms, I shall depreciate, hinder, or even destroy the spiritual development of my patients. And if I hold exclusively to a spiritual interpretation, then I shall misunderstand and do violence to the natural man in his right to exist as a physical being…The modern psychologist occupies neither the one position nor the other, but finds himself between the two." (1969c, 352)

Jung locates the analyst's position between the two worlds of spirit and sense in order to unite them in consciousness, and he located what I call the developed soul in the same position—between the two worlds. Let's examine the structure of the soul according to Jung's psychology, beginning with the first stage of its development in the functional soul complex.

The Structure of Soul

Soul as Functional Complex

The structure of the soul in Jung's psychology, as with Plato's philosophy, has a lower part that descends into the world of sense, in Jung's case into the ego and its complexes. He called this stage the functional soul. Soul as functional complex is similar to Plato's sensible man in that both organize experience through the impacts of the outer world. According to Jung, a person immersed in the ego complexes lives in his or her outer nature, heavily influenced by outer or collective events, and little able to reflect on inner realms. A person mostly conscious in the various unintegrated ego complexes is often filled with the conflicts related to passion and appetite, and driven to react to circumstances or fulfill desires even if they are destructive. It is a moment-to-moment life disposed to "character splitting" (Jung 1971, p. 464), by which Jung means the typical alterations of personality or multiple personalities that emerge according to external stimuli in a person organized at this level. Jung says that "such a man has no real character at all: he is not *individual* (q.v.) but *collective* (q.v), the plaything of circumstance and general expectations" (p. 465).

In its initial stage, soul progresses from one complex to another until a person is developed enough to consciously bear a valence of opposites together in an equal collaboration of the conscious and unconscious. Jung refers to this first stage of soul as "functional soul," locating it in complexes reflected in ego consciousness.

I have been compelled, in my investigations into the structure of the unconscious to make a conceptual distinction between *soul* and *psyche*. By psyche I understand the totality of all psychic processes, conscious as well as unconscious. By soul, on the other hand, I understand a clearly demarcated functional complex that can best be described as a "personality." (p. 463)

Soul has a normal tendency to alter or split at the functional complex stage because of the activation of complexes, when attention is captured by the contents of the complex. Caught in the shifting contents of the complex triggered by outer experience or an unconscious reaction, a person is prevented from a deeper realization or unity in the psyche.

A complex is a cluster of personal experiences that are organized around a particular archetype because they are linked to that archetype, for example experiences of being mothered collect around the mother archetype. A complex structures the psyche by linking together and organizing concrete experience on one level (the ego) while providing the connection to the transcendent archetype and universal life on a deeper, higher level. Acquired and activated through life experience, each complex is necessary for development. Complexes are the personality (also called the ego) and the personality is multiple rather than singular being divided in consciousness although held together by a background force. Jung says of the ego:

> For all its appearance of unity, it is obviously a highly composite factor. It is made up of images recorded from the sense-functions that transmit stimuli both from within and from without, and furthermore of an immense accumulation of images of past processes. (Jung 1969c, 323)

Ego consciousness is "a synthesis of the various 'sense-consciousnesses,' in which the independence of each separate consciousness is submerged in the unity of the overruling ego" (1969c, 324). Although each part is submerged within the overruling ego or personality, it is an unconscious unity (which eventually becomes conscious in the next stage of soul's development). Conscious experience of the ego is organized initially around the splitting and divisions of the complexes. This is necessary for development, as the divisions of the ego complexes provide the material for individual growth and evolution. Individuation (conscious development) is impossible without the complex.

The ego complexes in the human psyche include the unconscious and conscious realms. The unconscious includes the personal unconscious, which holds all the personal experience in every complex. It is also the super-conscious, the living realm of archetypes whose center is the Self, (the God-image and God proper). The archetypal realm remains mostly unconscious until it is apprehended through the work of individuation, when it can be felt. The personal content of the complexes occurs moment to moment in conscious attention before it is relegated to the personal unconscious.

Building the complexes that become personality and ego happens naturally. From birth onward experience passes into the unconscious where it fills in the complex, which begins empty of content. During this process a person is primarily aware of the flow of immediate experience. This is true throughout life although memory is also accessible when desired. The next stage of human consciousness includes the flow of attention but goes beyond into developing a capacity for reflection, a self-observation of the complex itself and the accumulated experiences that have shaped it—including the affects involved. This work of observing the complex leads to transformation of consciousness (see Chapter Four on the transcendent function).

Since Jung put soul at its initial stage in the functional complex and complexes congregate around an archetype, we know that while soul is a functional complex and thus unconscious of itself, it circles around the transcendent center of archetype and Self. Becoming conscious of functional soul involves becoming conscious of the significant complexes. Individuality begins to emerge in the work of making complexes conscious because that person begins to consider the truth or meaning of their life experience for themselves, outside of collective norms. Transforming awareness in the complex eventually resolves a significant degree of conflict in the complex, by uniting opposites. A person who has resolved a lot of conflict within his or her complexes feels and becomes aware of the numinous and collective reality of the archetype.

Soul's Progression

Soul's progression from its lower structure in functional complex to its higher structure as developed soul begins with the resolution of the Persona, the most evident "personality" or the outermost complex; the one that engages most prominently with the outer world. Remembering that the Persona is the idealized self, the persona complex is a "mask" made up of those contents a person wants to show the world. It is a mask because it hides the parts of the self that are undesirable. Jung says this complex is "'personal,' as opposed to 'individual'" (Jung 1971, 465). The human being still prone to the influence of the Persona is more identified with the collective or group experience of culture, rather than their own individuality. Living through the collective mask of the Persona, a person is heavily influenced by objects and attitudes that dominate culture in the outer world.

By reflecting inward and investigating the complex a person becomes acquainted with or discovers an unknown self that is alien and opposed to the conscious standpoint. Jung (1971, 466) remarks, "The subject, conceived as the 'inner object,' *is* the unconscious." When the unconscious complex becomes an object of study, the subjective self becomes an item for investigation. When this occurs, the usual attitude about the self and life shifts from looking outward through the persona, to looking inward and awakening "a personality...[that is] diametrically opposed to the outer personality" (p. 467).

The personality that emerges into awareness is called the shadow complex. The shadow, as opposed to the persona, does not accord with the ego ideal, or what a person thinks he or she is. Often this complex involves the wounds of childhood, traumatic states that remain protected and defended and remain in the "dark," or outside of awareness. Uniting the conflicts between the persona and shadow brings these two opposite complexes together. This union is a resolution that signals the progress of the functional soul from the persona/shadow to the anima/animus complex. Functional soul moves more deeply into the unconscious as each complex has adequate resolution.

The anima/animus complex produces a specific image that plays an important role in the development of soul. "Soul as anima" (Jung 1971, 467) is an image of the contra-sexual element, a man's feminine nature representing Eros or love. A woman's contra-sexual soul image is a male image called the animus, representing Logos or spirit. In *Two Essays* (1966, 210), Jung discusses at length specific qualities of these two aspects of the psyche. Some of what he says here is outdated, a natural artifact of his era, for example his portrait of a woman: "Her world, outside her husband, terminates in a sort of cosmic mist." I believe most contemporary women would bristle at such a characterization; I certainly do. In spite of this, Jung's genius in identifying the essential facts of the polarity between the feminine and masculine is still applicable, even essential.

When projected outward into the world, the images produced by the anima and animus lead to heterosexual relationship. The images appear in projection because integration of the complex has not been established. Although present in dreams as well as in projection, the actual projections onto the heterosexual partner can create conflict and hopefully a pressing need to examine and resolve it. Without the investigation to resolve conflict and therefore discover the anima and animus in the unconscious, the relationship will probably end in difficulty. Recollecting the projection of the contra-sexual image from the partner and integrating it into the self transforms it from one form to another. The projected image is part of an opposite pair in the complexes while the recollected image, because integrated, rises to the level of a function in the psyche.

The integrated anima and animus function in the psyche in the elevated role of "psychopomp" (Jung 1969a, 16), meaning a gateway to the unconscious. These essential yet usually unconscious aspects of the psyche are needed for wholeness in both the man and woman:

A mediator between the conscious and the unconscious … the anima becomes, through integration, the Eros of consciousness, so the animus becomes a Logos; and in the same way that the anima gives relationship and relatedness to a man's consciousness, the animus gives to the woman's consciousness a capacity for reflection, deliberation, and self knowledge. (p. 16)

More difficult to understand and explore than the shadow, the anima and animus are mostly unknown to the ordinary person. Deeper in the psyche then the persona and shadow, Jung believes the anima/animus have a "central position" (1969a, 21) and personify the entire unconscious itself. He says the anima and animus "filter the contents of the collective unconscious through to the conscious mind" (p. 20). Therefore, Jung identifies the whole unconscious as stamped by the contra-sexual aspect. "Woman is compensated by a masculine element and therefore her unconscious has, so to speak, a masculine imprint" (p. 14). Out of the four psychic functions, thinking, feeling, sensing, and intuition, the inferior functions (the functions that are more unconscious) are filtered through the contra-sexual imprint.

The anima/animus archetypes are "guardians of the threshold" (Jung 1966, 210) (a term Jung borrows somewhat reluctantly from theosophy) because they are the bridge to the unconscious. When the anima and animus are in their unintegrated, projected state, the person is mostly conscious of the outer world. Upon integration, the contents of the anima and animus complexes become a bridge to the unconscious because once the projection is withdrawn, it is known as the individual, inner, contra-sexual image. Relating to their own interior self-image, a person begins to understand that this image belongs to their own being and furthermore, that when it was projected, it functioned to defend against interior conflicts and fantasies. Through understanding projection and the previously hidden conflicts, the opposites in the complex can be united, ultimately releasing the anima or animus to serve its vital function as mediator between the conscious and unconscious standpoints.

The projective process is unavoidable and stretches across a spectrum from healthy relating to more destructive effects. For example, the healthy end of the spectrum provides for empathy, when a person projects their understanding and identification with the other person's experience. Therapeutic work usually involves the more destructive end of the projective process, where affective trauma's one is not aware of are projected onto someone else, and experienced as if they were coming from that other person. This process is the source of much suffering, and many interpersonal and cultural difficulties.

When the anima and animus are made conscious as the internal, contra-sexual images belonging to the individual, and therefore have become intentional paths to the unconscious mind, another level of development begins. The most significant opposites in human experience, the unifying of this male/female polarity is a wholeness symbolized by the "hermaphrodite" (Jung 1968a, 173), a "union of the strongest and most striking opposites" (p. 173). The hermaphrodite is a subject that is both male and female; a *coniunctio* or union likened to the divine marriage (p. 175). Jung has introduced a psychological process in the union of the anima and animus that advances and clarifies past efforts to signify the fundamental nature of the marriage of the feminine and masculine (p. 177).

A person who has transformed the anima/animus is "beyond division by sex" (1967a, 139) and therefore has made a leap onto a higher level of being, a higher degree of wholeness. This transformation is expressed in mundane terms through a self-aware and balanced relationship with oneself and an intimate partner. In extra-mundane terms, the unifying of the anima/animus in consciousness occasions a transformation of soul, an energetic leap forward out of the functional complex into its higher structure, which is a more developed state. Jung refers to this state as the "mysterium coniunctionis," meaning the self experienced as a nuptial union of opposite halves" (1969a, 64). The mysterious conjunction of the male-female opposition creates the seat or mirror where the reflection of the Self-symbol or God image occurs; not the complexes where the oppositions were originally experienced, and not the archetype which remains autonomous, or the Self that is an infinite totality so can only be experienced according to the limits or bounded nature of the created being.

The integration symbolized by the hermaphrodite is what Jung referred to as a third thing in the psyche. Bridging the ordinary and spiritual, this third is the gateway to consciousness of the transcendent realm of the archetype and the Self. Finding this gateway virtually unknown to western man, Jung nevertheless determines that it is necessary, calling it "the union of opposites through the middle path … It is at once the most individual fact and the most universal, the most legitimate fulfillment of the meaning of the individuals life" (1966, 205). Let's go on and explore how union through the "middle path" or third defines the process of finding the soul, and is the transformation that defines the individual.

Soul in the Third

When Jung moves away from placing soul in anima and animus, he is no longer using the term "soul" in its technical sense as a functional complex. In a long footnote in *Psychology and Alchemy,* the editors make distinctions in the translation of Jung's use of the word soul, i.e., soul as functional complex, as soul-image (referring to the psychic fact, numinous aspects of the transcendent psyche that appear in phenomenological experience), and soul as a transcendental concept akin to the Christian concept of soul (Jung 1968b, 9). Jung's soul, like Plato's, transforms and develops. It begins as a functional complex and in its progression develops a capacity to know the transcendent divine, so reflects a Christian context, which will become clearer as we go on.

Assimilating Jung means coming to terms with many contradictions found throughout the *Collected Works,* and his work on the stages of soul, especially the stage that has progressed past the functional complex, expresses these contradictions. Although the nature of the self and the psyche is a constant theme for Jung, in his work on the soul as functional complex and even more evident in his work on the developed soul as the individual self, he scatters his assertions throughout the volumes of his work, and therefore does not clarify and unify these various declarations into a coherent, consistent picture of soul as the individual self.

I bring together the various statements Jung has made about the individual soul in the third, resolving contradictions by making connections among his assertions. When Jung makes a theoretical leap from soul as functional complex to something else without a sequential narrative clarifying how it transforms or what it becomes, he leaves an important aspect of his theory of self/Self unclear. His assertions about this higher stage of soul describe an entity that straddles the ego and the complexes and the archetype of the Self; an entity that is a third located between the transcendent and the physical worlds. It is non-ego, goes beyond the ego and its complexes, is spirit, emerges from the union of opposites so is the result of the integration of the ego, and yet is not the archetype or the totality of the Self since these are both living, autonomous, transcendent beings that cannot be contained in an individual, nor are they the individual self.

Unifying Jung's presentation of the developed soul highlights and emphasizes its actual nature, function, and importance. Rather than accepting the lack of a defined, central premise concerning the reality of soul as the developed individual, in this next chapter I bring his statements about the second stage of soul into a coherent, consistent, well-defined ontological entity, which we will see has a Platonic root.

For Jung, soul is the dimension of the psyche or human being where the totality of the Self can be experienced and thus the spiritual or whole man can emerge or individuate. This "place" or part of the human being is no longer located in the complex but is instead located in-between the Self in the transcendent realm and the ego complexes in the natural world. Akin to Plato's view of the soul, Jung's view of the soul in the third unites all the worlds within, is an entity that is different from the combination of opposites that made it, and is not the ego complexes (sense), the Self (the One), or an archetype (form).

The Discrimination of Opposites

The discrimination and then the union of the opposites in the ordinary human being awaken a person to soul in the third. Jung describes it in Symbolic Life:

> The human personality is incomplete so long as we take simply the ego, the conscious, into account. It becomes complete only when supplemented by the unconscious. Therefore knowledge of the unconscious is indispensable for every true self-investigation. Through its integration, the centre of the personality is displaced from the limited ego into the more comprehensive self, into that centre which embraces both realms, the conscious and the unconscious, and unites them with each other. This self is the mid-point about which the true personality turns. (1980, 819)

Spiritual transformation happens in the "midpoint" and displaces the ego. A new center that is more comprehensive than the ego becomes the center of consciousness. Although Jung initially says this comprehensive entity is the Self, two sentences later he reidentifies this new center as a "midpoint," implying somewhere between the two extremes or opposites of ego and Self, the conscious (ego) and the unconscious (archetype and Self). This "true personality," if it is at the midpoint as Jung says, is in-between the ego and unconscious and is not an archetype or the totality of the infinite realization of the Self, as a subject is still implied. The two aspects of the psyche, the bounded or limited human consciousness and the infinite totality of the Self, united yet separate, are the subject and object joined in the midpoint of the true personality.

In *Two Essays* Jung repeats this description of soul in the middle or third when discussing the resolution of the complexes and their archetypes (1966, 229). He mentions the anima and animus, the great mother and the magician, and especially the "mana" or transcendent power or energy that is negotiated in the resolution of opposites. In a healthy accommodation of the opposites, the power does not belong to the conscious or unconscious parts of the person but instead becomes established between the two worlds. In this balance,

> The mana must have fallen to something that is both conscious and unconscious or else neither. This something is the desired "midpoint" of the personality, that ineffable something betwixt the opposites or else what unites them, or the result of conflict, or the product of energic tension: the coming to birth of personality, a profoundly individual step forward. (Jung 1966, 230)

Here Jung clearly identifies the individual, the true personality in the midpoint. It is Jung's soul birthed in the in-between third, no longer inhabiting the functional complex. In another place, Jung says essentially the same thing about the necessary consequences of uniting conflict: "no longer hid[ing] the conflict behind a mask. It requires a real solution and necessitates a third thing in which the opposites can unite … the resolution of opposites is always an energic process … something that expresses both sides" (1970b, 495). In the *Archetypes and the Collective Unconscious* he says it again: "Out of this collision of opposites the unconscious psyche always creates a third thing … which the conscious mind neither expects nor understands." (1968a, 167)

The true personality that emerges out of the conflicting opposites in the complexes in the middle or third cannot be understood by the conscious ego. It is that which "is no longer imprisoned in the petty, oversensitive, personal world of the ego, but participates freely in the wider world of objective interests…no longer the touchy, egotistical bundle of personal wishes, fears, hopes, and ambitions" (1966, 178). This true personality is unified with the ego complex rather than being the ego complex because it is conscious of the past conditions, of the opposites that have been united. Beyond the natural world and ego and yet not entirely the Self, this individual, true personality is attained through the difficult work of bringing together opposing parts within.

As we have seen, Jung refers to the displacement of the ego by the third in the middle when implying the individual soul, but in *Mysterium Coniunctionis* he refers to it as a replacement: "The new centre of personality which replaces the former ego" (1970, 494). The replacement of the ego does not mean its annihilation, rather the ego is joined to the new center so is still operating and providing experience to the whole: it is the "assimilation of the ego to a wider personality" (1969c, 292). In another discussion, describing the new center of soul, Jung examines an image executed by a patient where the disparate parts of the ego are contained by a "non-ego centre … that sort of ball or globe in the middle" (1976, 178). While identifying the non-ego center in the middle as the Self, he calls it a mandala, a holy place, and a temenos (p. 178). It is a receptacle or vessel that unifies all the disparate elements of the personality. This passage illustrates Jung's contradictions by implying it is the Self in the middle while in other places described previously, he points to a new personality, which cannot be the Self. Since Jung has already identified that integration of opposites occurs in a new third center of personality, we know it is not the ego in the middle. Since this midpoint is a non-ego center that is also a personality, it cannot be the totality of the Self. It must be the soul or third that reflects the totality of the Self within the bounded nature of the individual, which is more developed than the ego.

In another example of Jung referencing the Self while saying it is a personality in the middle, thus implying individuality rather than a totality, he says that the non-ego self is "a point midway between the conscious and the unconscious. This would be the point of new equilibrium, a new centering…ensur[ing] for the personality a new and more solid foundation" (1966, 221). This foundation is "the attainment of a newer and higher level of consciousness" (Jung 1968a, 263). What Jung seems to mean is that the Self is the source of this higher consciousness yet it is experienced in a personality (so is not the Self), yet since it is the attainment of a higher consciousness, it is not the personal ego and complex. It is an entity that conceives, apprehends, and understands beyond what the ego and complex is capable of, yet it is still a subject. All of this new, "higher" and more integrated experience includes the assimilated ego and the various complexes but is not identical with it.

Jung identifies consciousness as a precondition for the ego (1969c, 323). The consciousness existing prior to the ego is the spiritual world, and this spiritual world, according to Jung, has a potential individual center, a non-ego dimension that can become conscious of archetype, Self, and ego. This entity necessarily has to transcend the previous limits of the ego while still existing as an experiencing subject. It follows that soul is this subject, providing continuity of identity beyond the ego and so is pre-existent to the ego, as is the archetype and Self. Jung says consciousness "maintains the relation of psychic content to the ego"

(1971, 421-422), psychic content meaning the personal unconscious and the spiritual or psychic fact (psychic fact being the numinous content of archetype and Self experienced in the psyche).

The relation between the Self and ego is sustained by the soul, a level of being that is a unifying and cohesive force, pre-existing the ego and its acquired complexes, containing the ego, and connecting the higher and lower dimensions. It is the soul's relation to higher consciousness that allows for the reflection of divine life in physical reality. It is this divine reflection of the Self in soul that "perfects every nature in its individuality (the key word here being individuality) and thus makes man whole" (Jung 1969a, 185). Wholeness cannot be reflected in the complexes due to the separation of the opposites. It is when the opposites are united that higher consciousness can be reflected in the new center of personality or soul in the third.

Jung refers to the latent or unconscious soul as the individual in contrast to the acquired complexes in several places: "the individual disposition…is innate, and not acquired" (1971, 529), and "a man still is what he always was, and so he already is what he will become" (1969b, 258). Also, "The individual self…is inborn in each of its members" (1971, 376), and "*individuality,* has an *a priori* unconscious existence" (p. 447). This individuality of soul is the pre-existing condition of consciousness for the ego.

Always unique and individual, and simultaneously eternal and immortal, the developed spiritual soul exists in the transcendent or archetypal world in a dynamic relationship with the Self. Jung says, "The relation between the creator and the created is a *dialectical* one" (Jung 1967b, 60), dialectic referring to finding the truth among the opposites, which is unity of those opposites. He also makes a distinction between the Self and the soul that emphasizes that the Self cannot be the limited subject when he describes that the Self, God image, or God proper "cannot be localized in any individual" (1969a, 167), and, "strictly speaking, the (small) self must be regarded as the extreme opposite of God" (1969b, 190). At the same time Jung says the two share a unity: "as individual [the self] is smaller than small [and] as equivalent of the cosmos, [it] is bigger than big" (1968a, 171). Although the individual is smaller than small, it "forms the counterpart to the divine" (1968b, 25). In *Civilization in Transition,* Jung insists that the individual "never at any time takes the place of God, though it may… be a vessel for divine grace," a comment that points to the reflection of the Self in the soul. (1970, 463) The individual aspect of the Self (Jung says) "is precisely that which can *never be merged with the collective*" (my italic) (1966, 289). Such an important distinction between the individual and the Self underlines the existence of Jung's non-ego entity or new personality as the developed soul in the third

Soul in the third exists prior to one's being conscious of it. Jung says that the parts of the ego "need a powerful cohesive force to hold them together, and this we have already recognized as a property of consciousness" (1969c, 323). This cohesive force is the individual soul; a spiritual consciousness that is a non-ego consciousness separate from the ego that holds its disparate parts together and connects it to a wider psychic world. All these dynamics of soul create the potential for metaconsciousness: of becoming conscious of consciousness, some-thing the ego lacks since meta-consciousness requires two different levels of being. Jung differentiates the hierarchy of being into ego and soul several times, but in this example he says it directly: "The ego is a complex that does not comprise the total human being" (p. 324). Remembering Jung's assertions earlier of the individual human being never being the collective, we can understand that Jung is referring here to soul as the individual, not the Self.

When Jung comments that the source of ego-consciousness "might be conceived as a higher or wider consciousness in which the ego would be seen as an objective content … our ego-consciousness might well be enclosed within a more complete consciousness like a smaller circle within a larger" (1969c, p. 325), he refers to the hypostasis or creation of being. Uniting Jung's comments about the dimensions of the spiritual hierarchy, we can understand that the small circle of the ego is encompassed first by the non-ego third or soul, which is encompassed by the archetype. Finally, all levels of being are within the circle of the Self.

Jung describes the spiritual world as "living being" (1969c, p. 326), dimensions of the psyche that have been arbitrarily divided from the earthly body by our era of rational science, and are therefore unknown. Jung says spiritual experiences "denote an object of psychic experience which cannot be proved to exist in the external world and cannot be understood rationally" (p. 329). Spiritual experience of "living being" is a "psychic fact" (p. 328) and constitutes the in-breaking of transcendent worlds into individual perception. The Self and the archetypes break-in to experience through the intermediary of soul, since as I said earlier, the opposites in the complex cannot reflect the unity of the whole. Paranormal experiences and numinous experiences of the divine are examples of the "psychic fact" or living being breaking into phenomenological experience. Distinguishing the hierarchy of the spirit above the ego, Jung declares "our ego consciousness is not the only sort of consciousness in our system" (p. 333).

> If we are to do justice to the essence of the thing we call spirit, we should really speak of a "higher" consciousness rather than of the unconscious, because the concept of spirit is such that we are bound to connect it with the idea of superiority over the ego-consciousness. (1969c, 335)

Superior to the ego while providing the cohesive background that holds it together, this higher consciousness is a separate system from the ego as well as the source of spiritual experiences. Archetype and Self are higher consciousness existing beyond the ego but so is the non-ego center that Jung has identified as the individual that is inborn, and cannot dissolve into the collective. The inborn, awakened soul who has emerged due to some unity in the complexes supplies each person with the particulars required for actualizing their whole self, which are mirrored in soul's relationship to the transcendent archetype and Self. The awakened soul is a "wider consciousness [that] would be an image of the whole man" (1969c, 333). The Self is the unity or totality of the cosmos and represents wholeness in the human, but this wholeness must be received within the bounds of human experience. Therefore, the "whole man" must be something both individual and universal, and the ego lacks the universality while the collective lacks individuality. It is the third in-between that offers both.

The Union of Opposites

The Self in its universality provides each person with a potentially whole, individual life, yet the ego does not communicate this wholeness or individuality. The ego complex does not function in this way. Instead, Jung identifies a unity of the central complex that moves soul from the functional complex into something else. What emerges from the functional complex in this union of opposites is a different entity, a more developed entity; it is soul functioning in the third as the seat where transcendent knowledge can be felt.

The Self sends transcendent, teleological forces into human experience, leading a person who is stuck in the opposites towards realizing soul. These calls to growth enter ego consciousness through unconscious soul even if it appears to approach through an external event. "When the wider consciousness sees fit, a compelling idea is put before the ego-consciousness as an unconditional command … anyone who is conscious of his guiding principle knows with what indisputable authority it rules his life" (1969c, 335). The guiding principle of Self, mirrored in soul whether conscious or unconscious, leads the suffering ego towards addressing conflict. Ego's parts come together as this work proceeds, and as it proceeds and opposites connect, they become something else besides the ego; a third thing. The ego's system cannot touch the transcendent realm on its own. The whole Self guides individual growth by creating a conscious relationship between the soul and its lost or prodigal part, the incarnated ego.

The totality of the spirit reflected in the individual who is working on becoming the "whole man" includes all the psychic categories of ego and complex, the personal unconscious, the soul, the spiritual world of archetype, and the Self. Jung feels that the human relationship to spirit or the experience of the "psychic fact" (1969c, 328), "needs completing and perfecting through life" (p. 336), meaning the spirit needs to be developed, unified, and balanced in conscious life. This happens through the transcendent function where ego consciousness becomes soul consciousness. Jung says the spirit is "a treasure hard to attain [that] lies hidden in the ocean of the unconscious" (1968b, 117). Spirit cannot be attained without the successful assimilation of the unconscious. This assimilation is a transformation that takes consciousness out of its previous home into the larger, wider consciousness of soul. It is an

alteration of the ego as well as of the unconscious contents. Although it is able to preserve its structure, the ego is ousted from its central and dominating position and thus finds itself in the role of a passive observer who lacks the power to assert his will under all circumstances … That is the ego cannot help discovering that the afflux of unconscious contents has vitalized the personality, enriched it and created a figure that somehow dwarfs the ego in scope and intensity. (1969c, 224)

This enriched figure dwarfs the ego in its capacity to realize higher consciousness. Jung differentiates this enriched figure from pathological states, and also from the negative consequences of a poor assimilation of the unconscious, such as the inflated ego identified with the Self. The avoidance of these poor results he identifies with the "scintilla, the soul spark, the little wisp of divine light that never burns more brightly than when it has to struggle against the invading darkness" (1969c, 225). It is the strength of the inborn soul, found in the point of attention that when focused on the complex, goes against the darkness of unconscious conflict. In this passage, Jung finds the scintilla a soul spark while in other places he contradicts this and makes it an archetype (1970b, 490). When Jung identifies the scintilla as the soul spark, he means the scintilla is light from the Self and not the totality of the Self.

In discussing the alchemical union of opposites in *Mysterium Coniunctionis,* Jung refers to substances that represent a metaphor for developing consciousness or individuation. The final stage of this work with these substances results in a non-ego entity, a new center of personality that mirrors the Self but is not the Self:

> The whole of the conscious man is surrendered to the self, to the new centre of personality which replaces the former ego. Just as, for the mystic, Christ takes over the leadership of consciousness and puts an end to a merely ego bound existence. (1970b, 494)

Here Jung begins by making the new center of personality equivalent with the Self and then identifies Christ as this new center, the developed individual soul who recognizes the divine Self at his or her own center and thus organizes his or her individual earthly life around that experience. In some places Jung identifies Christ as the symbol of the Self (1969a, 68); in other places he refers to Christ as the inner man (1970b, 491) ("man" being individual therefore distinct from the Self). Jung uses Christ as the model for individuation and the conscious individual soul because by mastering himself and assimilating the darkness of the human shadow with the divine light, Christ united the worlds and thereby transformed human consciousness from ego to soul.

Jung refers to Christ as the perfect man who achieves completion. The archetype of the Self symbolizes completion whereas Jung points out that it is the man who symbolizes perfection. The union of the perfect or whole man (Christ consciousness or soul consciousness) with its opposite (Jesus or the man of sense and ego complexes) is symbolized in the crucifixion (1969a, 68-69), which liberates the created Earth-bound ego and body into completion. Jesus becomes complete through transcendence in Christ consciousness through the paradox inherent in the union of opposites, which always signifies the transcendent realm (p. 69). The transcendent nature of this paradox in Christ involves the Self but is nevertheless not identical with it, nor does this transcendence happen in the ego.

Jung states it this way:

Where the archetype [of the Self] predominates, completeness is forced upon us against all our conscious strivings … The individual may strive after perfection … but must suffer from the opposite of his intentions … The Christ image fully corresponds to this situation: Christ is the perfect man who is crucified … the trans-cendental idea of the self that serves psychology as a working hypothesis can never match that image because, although it is a symbol, it lacks the character of a revelatory historical event. (1969a, 69)

Although Christ realizes the archetype of the Self, the Self cannot be identical with Christ because Christ was the revelatory event, the individuated version of the earthly Jesus who was an incarnate human being living a concrete existence within history. Rather, the Self is the divine energy symbolized and realized in the Christ, Jesus' complete, whole self or transcendent soul. Christ, Jesus' perfected soul, is a new, third, consciousness created from the unified opposites within Jesus. The correspondence or conjunction of opposites, both terms referring to the joining together or agreement of two things, i.e. unity of two things, always results in their annihilation (1969a, 70) and the anni-hilation of opposites signifies that they are no longer what they were, but instead have been transformed into something else. This something is no longer the ego and also not the Self. It is a new, third thing—symbolized for Jung and most Christians in Jesus Christ.

Jesus Christ's perfection and completion reflects the unity of opposites coming together within his own being. He united the macrocosm of the divine Self with the microcosm of the human self through his own consciousness. Although Jung recognizes the opposites in the quote below, he does not identify where the conjunction of opposites occurs.

> As a historical personage Christ is unitemporal and unique; as God, universal and eternal. Likewise the self: as the essence of individuality it is unitemporal and unique; as an archetypal symbol it is a God image and therefore universal and eternal. (p. 63)

The experience of the opposites coming together (Christ) results in a transcendent event, so it must be beyond the ego— in a non-ego part of the psyche. At the same time, it must occur in the human realm since experienced and described. An act of development contained within human experience, the Christ or the essence of individuality cannot be identical to the Self or God. It seems that the part and whole, the man and God, come together in something that is level of consciousness, which is epitomized in Jesus who became the transcendent Christ. Jung (1988a, 187) reports Jesus' soul (the Christ) appearing after the crucifixion to his disciples in a subtle body, and in doing so, awakens others to the same kind of development.

In *Aion* (1969a), Jung describes an ancient Gnostic teaching about the soul and Christ's role in human evolution:

> In unconscious humanity there is a latent seed that corresponds to the prototype Jesus. Just as the man Jesus became conscious only through the light that emanated from the higher Christ and separated the natures in him, so the seed in unconscious humanity is awakened by the light emanating from Jesus, and is thereby impelled to a similar discrimination of opposites. (pp. 64-66)

The Self or God can never be the same as the non-ego, individual soul, even though the small self or individual self "signifies man's likeness to God" (1970, 539). The individual and God, as Jung (1969c) asserts in the previous statements are different yet the same (a Platonic doctrine). They are "at one and the same time, absolute subjectivity and universal truth" (p. 230). Jung (1971) reminds us in *Psychological Types* that God is not "a single, constant being" (p. 46), but provides for "the absolute individuality of the self, [combining] uniqueness with eternity and the individual with the universal" (1968b, p. 19). The Self or God is One and many, unified yet divided, the same yet different. This is a Platonic doctrine that provides for the individual existence of soul in the third beyond the ego, in dual-unity with God—a dynamic discussed earlier concerning Plato's concept of soul that also exists in Jung's writings.

As we can see, Jung uses Christ as the symbol of individual, higher consciousness in order to point to a psychological reality that is distinct from the religious view. In this vein, Jung describes the psychological nature of the functional complex of the anima/animus in *Two Essays* (1966, 191) when he refers to its autonomy and its immortality as "simply a psychic activity that transcends the limits of consciousness." Autonomous to the ego and beyond death, Jung's idea of soul as anima and later when it becomes more developed, always "lives in a realm beyond the body" (Jung 1969c, 348). The psychological reality of soul, as well as its transcendence, suggests to Jung that it is "an invisible personal entity that apparently lives in a world very different from ours … it is but a step to imagining that this entity must lead an entirely independent existence, perhaps in a world of invisible things" (1966, 191). Jung's feeling that soul is a separate entity living beyond usual consciousness leads him to admit its objective truth and here he reclaims its religious function, saying, "There is some justification for the old view of the soul as an objective reality—as something independent and therefore capricious and dangerous" (1969c, 347). Capricious and dangerous because it is unconscious; the religious soul must become psychological in order to become conscious and thereby play its part in human evolution.

Becoming psychological, soul awakens and can then reflect its divine source, thus also becoming spiritual. As the eye is the primary channel through which we see the outer world, so Jung says the soul is the channel through which we see the spiritual world: "As the eye to the sun, so the soul corresponds to God" (1968b, 10). The eye takes in the light of the sun and the soul the light of the divine. The capacity of soul to realize the divine causes Jung to insist on its existence. He exclaims, "The soul cannot be 'nothing but.' On the contrary it has the dignity of an entity endowed with consciousness of a relationship to Deity" (p. 10). Furthermore, he adds "supreme values reside in the soul" (p. 13). Here Jung spells out what he often implies, namely, that soul is in relationship with the Self, rather than identified with it.

In another passage where Jung is explaining the alchemical practices of Dorn, in particular the combining of opposites, he initially says the entity in which the opposites come together is the Self, and then a few sentences later he describes the in-between soul in the third where the union of body and spirit takes place. In a typical contra-diction, in this quote Jung uses the term animus to represent spirit when in other places he uses it to describe the psychic image produced by the anima/animus complex when soul is in the functional complex. I adhere to the latter use, interpreting the spirit to mean the trans-cendent archetype and Self and the psychic image to be connected to the archetype and spirit but until realized, it remains unconscious.

> The spirit (*animus)*, which is to unite with the soul, he called a "spiracle [*spiraculum*] of eternal life" a sort of "window into eternity" …. Whereas the soul is an organ of the spirit and the body an instrument of the soul. The soul stands between good and evil and has the "option" of both. It animates the body by a "natural union," just as, by a "supernatural union," it is endowed with life by the spirit. (1970b, 471)

In the same discussion Jung describes soul in the third in almost identical terms: "soul animates the body, just as the soul is animated by the spirit" (1970, 472). Apparently soul animates the body even in the early stage of the functional complex. In the *Archetypes and the Collective Unconscious* (1968a), Jung equates the anima-soul with the nature of being itself: "Being that has soul is living being. Soul is the living thing in man, that which lives of itself and causes life" (p. 26). Here Jung unequivocally declares that it is soul, as a functional complex or developed in the third, that causes life in the body.

Uniting the opposites and becoming conscious in developed soul "puts an end to the conflict between mind and matter" (1969c, 353). Jung details some of the opposites that exist and must be brought to union in the soul. They are feeling and thinking (Jung 1971, 58), the conscious and unconscious (1966, 229; 1970b, 536), within and without (1966, 237), this world and the heavenly trinity (1969b, 177), spirit and matter, bright and dark (1970b, 536), and life and spirit (1969c, 337). Every instance where there is a union of opposites, something new and different is created; Jung calls it a "united double nature" (Jung 1970b, 29). This is akin to the dual-unity that I have experienced.

> The two opposites cancel each other out, their impact resulting –
> in accordance with the laws of energetics—in the birth of a third
> and new thing, a son who resolves the antagonism of the parents
> and is himself a "united double nature." (p. 29)

This united double nature or son who resolves the opposites is described through alchemy, and Jung also associates it closely with Christian transubstantiation, which symbolizes the Christ or Paraclete who brought spirit and matter together. Feminine matter and masculine spirit coming together symbolize the united double nature as does the Egyptian soul arising from the union of the masculine and feminine in the mother and father. Through these examples Jung illustrates the bringing together of the opposites in a united double nature, and the dynamic relationship of dual-unity at the center of the cosmology and of the soul.

Jung uses the united double nature of Plato's philosophy, of the alchemical opus, and of Christian symbolism to inform the dual-unity at the base of his own psychology. This dual-unity emerges consciously through the transcendent function starting with the resolution of the functional soul when the hermaphrodite or union of the anima and animus emerge into a new united double nature. The developed soul is the two and one together. Jung says it is a "self evident truth … only partially digested by the man of today" (1970b, 536) that "if a union is to take place between opposites … it will happen in a third thing, which represents not a compromise but something new" (1970b, 536).

Later on in the same paragraph Jung again identifies the soul in the third and its united double nature or dynamic of dual-unity. He says it is "man as he is, and the indescribable and super-empirical totality of that same man" (p. 536). The ultimate in opposites, the empirical ego and complex and the transcendent totality of the Self are brought together in the third, making the paradox of an apparent duality into a unity. The subject or individual soul who experiences the totality of the Self is both the same yet also different from its source, and it is also the same yet different from the opposites in the ego complexes that have been united.

In *The Symbolic Life* (1980, 734), Jung reiterates that the Self is the central archetype, and equates it with the Deity. He again uses Christ as the epitome of the whole man whose crucifixion represents the process of uniting the opposites. In this reference Christ is "the model for the human answers and his symbol is the cross, the union of the opposites" (p. 735). The work of seeing and understanding and thereby uniting the opposites in soul is the discovery of the "middle way," (p. 735), or individuation, which is a conscious journey back to unity. It is a "task left to man, and that is the reason why man is so important to God that he decided to become a man himself" (p. 735). Without the opposites of the complex experienced in the ego there is no material for transformation.

In examining the symbolism of the mandala in a patient's dream, Jung identifies a central point where unity of the conscious and unconscious opposites is achieved through reflection:

> Each side must perfectly balance the other as its mirror-image, and this image is to fall at the "central point" which evidently possesses the property of reflection … [it is] the point of intersection of two worlds that correspond but are inverted by reflection. (Jung 1968b, 171)

Carrying forward Jung's ideas of a united double nature, his statements that the individual self is never lost in the collective, and his assertions about a non-ego, new personality in the middle or third, it follows that this central point which brings together two worlds through reflection, is soul in the third. Reflection in the third inverts the two worlds, meaning they switch positions. The interior spiritual world becomes the center of experience instead of the ego, inverting the usual psychic process. Reflection is the act of looking at the subject as object—consciousness investigating the unconscious—instead of the usual perception of self as subject in relation to the external object. This inversion is the principal act of individuation, and therefore also of the transcendent function. Spirit becomes a known phenomenon through the transcendent function, not just a belief. Jung expressed his own knowledge of divine life:

> I am sufficiently convinced of the effects man has always attributed to a divine being … Either I know a thing and then I don't need to believe it; or I believe it because I am not sure that I know it. I am well satisfied with the fact that I know experiences which I cannot avoid calling numinous or divine. (1976, 707)

Through his own experience Jung knew that God existed. It is the individual that "knows," an entity that is not Self and also not ego. Along with the birth of consciousness of soul in the third ontological level is the transformation of experiencing the totality or the universe. Jung says it in reference to an analysis: "Consciousness of…

individuality should coincide exactly with the reactivation of an archaic god-image" (Jung 1966, 160). Paradoxically one's real, separate, and permanent spiritual individuality is experienced when one wakes up to God or the Self, in a conscious relationship of dual-unity.

The Dual-Unity of Soul in the Third

I have discussed the nature of dual-unity in the section on Plato's soul so you will recognize this relationship in the following discussion, among the particular psychological dimensions that belong uniquely to Jung. To review, dual-unity is the dynamic that allows for unity or merging simultaneously with differentiation or separateness. It is a state of consciousness where two beings and levels of being experience unity or oneness without either losing their separate identity. This cosmic architecture organizes or structures the universe and the psyche, as well as creates the levels of consciousness in hypostasis. It makes the human soul unique among all beings because through dual-unity, soul in the third has the potential to realize the whole universe within.

Through the aspect of unity, higher being "participates" (remembering Plato) in the human soul—thus soul is one with and can experience the divine while continuing to form and organize its own life. Likewise, soul "participates" in the ego's level of experience and is thus one with the ego while ego continues its own life. The aspect of duality is what creates the uniqueness of every being or individual. Because the duality of dual-unity is fundamentally transformed by the unity associated with it, there is no true duality in soul or in the universe.

Dual-unity in soul creates mental and emotional stability because of the trust that emerges within the individual self for one's own higher spiritual form, which receives light from its unity with the divine whole. Soul, the small inner voice that is rarely heard among the clamor of the ego until some degree of individuation has occurred, guides and supports the ego through the changes and challenges of the world. The ultimate term of the developed soul is experience of the Self or God constantly informing and containing a balanced, harmonious, and fully embodied life in the ego and physical world. Developing the soul is a life-long project and few attain the stability of constant presence to the Self or God.

The dynamic of dual-unity is what allows conscious union of the hierarchical dimensions of being. This movement towards unity is circular, beginning with awareness in ego experience which is lifted through integration into incremental consciousness in the third increasing the degree of realization of the divine Self in soul. This realization is then felt as heightened awareness and experience in the ego.

The Self or God cannot be known in the divided state of the ego in the same way that occurs in the developed soul. Belief in God belongs to ego, as do numinous flashes of transcendent life. Experience and knowledge of the Self and God belongs to soul, as does more persistent transcendent realization. The ego can reach beyond simple belief by becoming aware of the momentary numinous or peak experiences of the archetype and Self. This is a valuable attribute and it happens at various times in all persons. This flash is a deep, wordless knowing of the mystical reality behind appearances. It is a deeply personal experience matching one's own temperament and proclivities, so if one is an outdoor type it may occur through nature, if a musical person perhaps through music. In each case it is a momentary unveiling of the transcendent Self or God. Following this mystical flash forward into the work of individuation leads to more stable experience of the numinous dimension and a relationship with God or the Self.

The idea of an absolute unity with the archetype of the Self or God while embodied or after death implies a total abandonment of any separate individuality. However, consciousness of unity, by its very nature, must include every step and state that occurs on the way. This "way" is an individual and thus differentiated path that when created, is always part of the whole so is never destroyed whether one is conscious of it or not. Rather, the individual soul and God exist as two and one in a simultaneous experience of relationship, of differentiation as well as Oneness. This is the dual-unity at the heart of soul.

The archetypes, have their own dual-unity, existing as single entities in the psyche as well as in a unity in the archetypal realm. This mirrors the dual-unity of the parts of the ego complexes, which begin as opposite parts in the unconscious and are eventually brought together into some degree of conscious, integrated unity. The archetypes also exist in dual-unity with the Self or Deity—the central archetype appearing within each single archetype and both existing in dual-unity with the complexes—since they appear in the center of every complex Being distinct from soul ontologically, the archetype is not the individual in transformation capable of spanning all the dimensions from ego to the divine. Instead, it remains eternally in the archetypal realm even when realized within the being of the individual. It has its own specific being and phenomenology. One feature of this pheno-menology is the archetype's role in forming and organizing personal experience within the ego. Another feature is its numinous influence on the ego, which can lead to intentional effort towards individuation, and therefore the numinous light of consciousness in developed soul.

The archetype is an entirely divine being and is unlike the human individual because the human has the divine as its highest aspect and the animal as its lowest. Bringing the divine dimension into the biological animal through the dual-unity of the developed human soul enlightens and balances the animal or biological self, which is hence-forth guided by the higher life. Attaining conscious dual-unity in the soul is a unique achievement because in its wake, one can realize the cosmos. Although the archetype and ego play their parts, it is the dual-unity of soul that enables this experience.

When conscious dual-unity is achieved in soul, soul brings whole-ness to the divine and at the same moment the divine brings wholeness to the individual soul. The dual-unity of the soul's structure in the third allows for reflection and experience in a higher being that does not descend through the aspect that does. The two levels of Being separate and unite simultaneously and thus experience the act of creation reciprocally. Jung often describes the duality of the psyche in ego and Self while at the same time declaring it a whole or unity. These two different attitudes in Jung come together in the dynamic of dual-unity, which involves the soul in the third. For example, Jung states, "The conscious mind is usually reluctant to see or admit the polarity of its own background, although it is precisely from there that it gets it energy" (1970b, xvii). The background to the conscious mind is of course the unconscious. Energy is sustained in the opposition between the two, and is released into a new form when they are united.

I am sure it is clear by now that doing the work of uniting opposites within brings into awareness an experience of the unconscious. Subsequently, the unconscious can be realized and known in the soul. Jung says the process "entails an almost unbearable tension because of the utter incommensurability between conscious life and the un-conscious process, which can be experienced only in the innermost soul and cannot touch the visible surface of life at any point" (1968b, 146). Soul's capacity to experience both higher and lower worlds from its in-between position prompts Jung to say in *Psychology and Alchemy* "soul possesses a religious function" (1968b, 13) because it can realize the divine in a way the ego cannot. Jung (1969b, 280) invokes Christ again in this context: "Subjective consciousness is united with an objective centre, thus producing the unity of God and man represented by Christ." In addition to Christ being the epitome of the developed soul in the third; here, Jung refers to the dual-unity of Christ and God— two brought together into a one.

The dynamic of dual-unity is the organizing force behind the transformation of energy and consciousness from one ontological level to another. This happens in the transcendent function, which is the cornerstone of Jung's psychology. Let's now go on to examine the process of individuation and what role the transcendent function plays in producing awareness of soul in the third.

Individuation and the Transcendent Function

Jung declares, "Without the experience of the opposites there is no experience of wholeness and hence no inner approach to the sacred figures" (1968b, 20). This statement describes the process of individuation, which begins with the separation of opposites in complexes. Separation occurs as a necessary imposition upon primal, collective, unconscious unity in order to form the personality. Later efforts at individuation bring about a conscious reunion of these opposites, and conscious experience of the transcendent sphere of the archetype and divine Self.

Individuation involves both teleology, or the inborn impulse or urge towards development, and entelechy. Teleology and entelechy explain the genesis of the individual. Entelechy means actuality rather than potentiality (which teleology is concerned with). It refers to the actual reality of the existing individual in an invisible, unconscious, or latent form. Jung (1968a, 77) says: "It looks as if something already existent were being put together. The newborn infant is endowed as a 'sharply defined individual entity,' which appears indeterminate …. because we cannot see it." The process of normal developmental growth (acquiring the personal material in the ego complexes) and then the effort of individuation (integrating the complexes) reveal the actualities that had been hidden in the unconscious soul.

The teleological force within the psyche draws a person towards actualizing their potential and inborn self. Entelechy is the unfolding of that hidden self as teleology acts upon the life experience, in order to guide it towards fulfillment. How does this fulfillment occur and how do the opposites become reunited in soul? Let's examine the little-discussed energetic aspect of the transcendent function, where energy is transformed from one form or category of being to another and the energy of the ego becomes soul in the third.

Transformation in the Transcendent Function

Jung (1969c, 405) said, "Life is an energy process. Like every energy-process, it is in principle irreversible and is therefore directed towards a goal." He also remarked earlier in the same text, "Psychic processes… can hardly be interpreted as anything but energy processes…a phenomenon of energy" (p. 233). Therefore, it stands to reason that any changes affected in the psyche are energetic. Jung describes this at the very beginning of his discussion, saying, "Some kind of energy underlies the changes in phenomena, [and] that it maintains itself as a constant throughout these changes" (p. 4). Experienced as life itself and inner motion and force, energy has "as many quantitative measurements and different forms as physical energy" (p. 7).

For Jung, energy begins with libido. Libido is "energy-value which is able to communicate itself to any field of activity whatsoever, be it power, hunger, hatred, sexuality, or religion" (Jung 1967b, 137). As such, it is "the creative power of our own soul" (p. 121) as well as universal being (p. 160). Jung also links libido with light expressing itself as "images of sun, light, fire, sex, fertility, and growth" (p. 221). It is compared to "a steady stream pouring its waters into the world of reality" (p. 173). The ultimate truth about libido is "we can only experience [it] through its effect on us…it is the unconscious creative force which wraps itself in images" (p. 222). Jung describes energy as equivalent to the Self, expressed at all levels of being and "a tension of opposites" (Jung 1969c, 55), a "living balance between opposites" (p. 55) as well as the "equilibration of all kinds of opposites" (p. 207). The energy of the psyche exists on a continuum from the archetype of the

Self and God to the complexes, which is a path from the deepest interior to the more external level of consciousness. Where energy is constellated determines the form in which it will appear, for example, "the archetype consists of both—form and energy" (1968a, 102).

Energy manifests in a continuum as the balance of opposites, and it also "immediately hypostatizes itself as the psychic forces (drives, affects and other dynamic processes)" (Jung 1969c, 30). It "appears to us in the form of sexual, vital, mental, [and] moral 'energy'" (p. 29). Thought, will, and affect are energy values. Thought, Jung conjectures, has its own energetic reality. "Thought *was* and *is*…even though it refers to no tangible reality, it has an effect…otherwise no one would have noticed it…thought may have left undeniable traces of reality behind it" (p. 383). Jung illustrates his point by ironically suggesting that

> we can produce a most devastating fact like the atom bomb with the help of this ever-changing phantasmagoria of virtually non-existent thoughts, but it seems wholly absurd to us that one could ever establish the reality of thought itself. (1969b, 480)

Jung's point is that although it seems esoteric or even occult, thought has an energetic and invisible reality of its own.

Will is "disposable energy" (Jung 1969c, 45), which becomes more available to a person as they become free from the life of instinct and efforts to survive. In *The Symbolic Life*, Jung (1980, 17) equates willpower with the energy of the ego. It is that energy that is responsible for function and action, first formed internally in intention and desire, then actualized. As willpower, energy is

> always experienced specifically as motion and force when actual, and as a state or condition when potential. Psychic energy appears, when actual, in the specific, dynamic phenomena of the psyche, such as instinct, wishing, willing, affect, attention, capacity for work… [and] when potential, energy shows itself in specific achievements,

possibilities, aptitudes, attitudes, etc. which are its various states. (1969c, 15)

For some people there is energy or will power (both actual and potential) available for the effort of individuation. Energy is deliberately transformed in the process of individuation, and therefore, so is consciousness.

How does energy transform? Living a natural life of instinct, energy is transformed along its natural gradient. Natural phenomena are produced, but no "work" (Jung 1969c, 41), work referring to individuation. In natural processes and in "work," "living matter is itself a transformer of energy" (p. 41), meaning that animate processes within the body produce energetic change, as does effort applied to the complex in individuation. Living matter or energy produces different effects according to intensity, which is related to the will (p. 25). Will influences all human functioning (p. 183) and has the power to overcome other forms of energy. Jung refers to the intensity of will overcoming other forms of energy as canalization. Canalization happens when will is intentionally used to channel energy into a specific direction. Jung says, "Canalization of libido...the process corresponding to the physical transformation of energy or conversion...[is] a transfer of psychic intensities or values from one content to another" (p. 41). Canalization provides for transformation of energy in the transcendent function, and this transformation of energy is at the heart of all change during the process of individuation.

In the course of individuation, the concentration of will on the unconscious produces "work," effort that lifts the natural process above its instinctual gradient into symbol formation. "With increasing freedom from sheer instinct...the intrinsic energy of the function ceases altogether to be oriented by instinct...and attains a so-called 'spiritual' form" (Jung 1969c, 182).

The canalization of libido or energy that happens through the transcendent function produces a spiritual form that involves not only the intensity of will, affect, and thought but also extensity. "The theory of energy recognizes not only a factor of *intensity*, but also a factor of *extensity*" (Jung 1969c, 20). Jung says that Hartmann (quoted in Jung 1969c, 21) explains, "The quantity, or the extensity factor, of energy is attached to one structure and cannot be transferred to another structure without carrying with it parts of the first; but the intensity factor can pass from one structure to another" (p. 20). The intensity factor is the degree or quality of concentrated attention a person has developed, which is commensurate to the strength of the will. As the power of attention develops through the early stages of individuation, the ego may not be strong enough to withstand the tension required for transformation. In this case, change does not occur above the natural gradient, and a person remains limited by an instinctual and unconscious life.

When a person has acquired the necessary stability of concentration and will, the ego can endure the tension of opposites as they unite in consciousness. The newly created energy produced through this union is then lifted above the natural gradient into a higher more unified level of being. Moving above the natural level of being, something of the old function/structures transfers to the new because of the extensity factor. This is important because the awakening of consciousness on the unified level still "knows" or experiences the instinctual and natural self. The old structure, consisting of the necessary parts of the complex, has been transferred to the more unified level. The intensity factor, or the degree of attention or concentration applied through the will to the originally opposed, unconscious complex expands into the new structure. The new structure is the developed soul in the third, a higher, more unified level of being than the complex. Soul in the third position has the capacity to unite with and mirror the transcendent archetype and the Self while maintaining its connection to the complex below. These dynamics express the conscious dual-unity of the developed soul achieved in the transcendent function.

The process of the transcendent function is as follows:

For this collaboration of opposing states to be possible, they must first face one another in the fullest conscious opposition…When there is full parity of the opposites, attested by the ego's absolute participation in both, this necessarily leads to a suspension of the *will*…Since life cannot tolerate a standstill, a damming up of vital energy results, and this would lead to an insupportable condition did not the tension of opposites produce a new, uniting function that transcends them…from the activity of the unconscious there now emerges a new content. (Jung 1971, 478-479)

The new content transcends the old, so is located on a higher ontological level. It emerges through the transcendent function from the previously opposed but now united complex. That new content (what was unconscious is now conscious) is an energetic substance (consciousness) that was previously centered in the opposites in the complex and is now united and centered in the developing soul. On a practical level, this new consciousness has the capacity to keep opposing realities in mind at once. Beyond this, there is a felt experience of soul and higher dimensions, a new meaning in the sense of a living wholeness, and a light or depth existing at the center of all phenomenon appears when consciousness remains more grounded in soul than ego.

The necessary suspension for transformation of the opposites occurs in the ego when the will holds opposing forces together rather than allowing expression of either side of the complex. Thus the will is put to work resisting the pressure to act out or identify with, in attitude, thought, and behavior, the repetitive, destructive patterns but also the natural patterns of opposition that can cause conflict in the complex. The suspension of the forces involved in withholding energy from either side of the complex while keeping both sides in mind at once (and therefore keeping the opposites together) liberates experience from the complex and thus the ego.

In the suspension of the will, one is purposely separating from and witnessing rather than investing in, identifying with, or acting out instinctual or ego-based impulse, desire, thought, and action. Suspending oneself from the opposing, conflicted, and defended content in the ego and even old patterns and habits that don't necessarily form symptoms but just prevent higher growth, releases energy from those structures. The old Freudian term "decathect" has valence as a reference in this instance, as the suspension in question is an actual withdrawal of energy from old structures. In the wake of this withdrawal, the newly available energy moves from the ego and complex into another form through the transcendent function. One gradually gets more conscious of the opposites through returning to work again and again on a particular conflict or opposition and this repetition eventually results in a transformation from one psychic structure to another. As increasing degrees of energy are transformed, consciousness grows in the third and commensurate degrees of archetypal and divine reality are mirrored and therefore felt in the soul. At this threshold, awareness of dual-unity in soul becomes a more permanent aspect of identity.

Growing consciousness in soul causes perception, experience, and understanding to shift from purely personal preoccupations to an experience of a deeper individuality, couched in a larger realization of the collective unfolding of human dynamics. The wider yet deeper perspective of the individual is from a more differentiated position, since one is no longer merged unconsciously in the collective. As a person becomes more uniquely individual, he or she becomes, paradoxically, more consciously united with the collective or whole.

Ego consciousness is by nature attached in function to the collective unconscious through the complexes (because there is an archetype at the center of every complex), and at this level the collective is instinctively experienced as undifferentiated and merged in personal experience. The effect of such an undifferentiated state produces a more or less unconscious orientation to self and others, and world or cosmos. Attention is most often applied to protecting the self, identifying with collective concerns, and the exterior aspects of life. The results of such an orientation—both positive and negative—prevent individuality from emerging. Individuality, or soul, is also by nature attached in function to the archetype. First, through its functional stage, it is attached to an archetype through its location in complexes. Then, developed soul is attached to the archetype through awareness of dual-unity, where soul can experience or be aware of the whole: the complex, the archetype, and Self. Through awareness of dual-unity in soul, an individual can become conscious of the collective in a differentiated unity.

The ability to realize this differentiated unity—dual-unity of soul—while living through an emotional event, to understand the underlying motivations of the event in one's own complexes, to experience the personal impact of the event without entirely identifying with it and therefore having some capacity to feel its archetypal reality, is dual-unity in action. The center of this dual-unity is the Self, anchoring one's inner experience in soul instead of the false center of security placed by the ego in itself and physical reality. Dual-unity produces a sense of security that can only be felt through experience of spirit, the divine whole that always accompanies one through life. Consciousness of dual-unity in soul produces a deep sense of being in physical life but not of it. The subtlety of this level of being increases sensitivity to experience rather than decreases it. Dual-unity is not detachment from life and the world; it is a measure of freedom that exists within while one experiences a deeper level of relationship and activity.

Freedom consists in soul's awareness of its own nature and place in the cosmos because the numinous reality of the divine exists as a felt quality within and behind every personal event. While pain, grief, and trauma rise and fall in the psyche, the quality of spiritual depth shaping experience deeply tempers locally staged events. This numinous quality that accompanies the awareness of soul is acquired incrementally, as is all developmental growth. When one observes how long it took to acquire the complexes, one can understand how long it may take to acquire the grace of divine light in the soul. In my experience, this grace, realized within, does not protect one from the fears and tensions sometimes involved in outer events, but provides a steady ground of connection and support. Many in today's world seem to think this state can be experienced without effort and discipline. What is important to understand is that development of the Self takes will and attention.

Consciousness of soul in the third liberates experience because of the existential freedom that is individuality. There are several attributes of the evolved soul or individual self that differentiate experience from that of the complexes and personal unconscious, and those are the values associated with spiritual consciousness. For example, these attributes include compassion, empathy, understanding, acceptance, love for all being, flexibility, respect, kindness and responsibility for oneself. Also, generosity, presence, peacefulness, calmness, contentment, the ability to handle conflict without acting out and anger without being destructive. The capacity to see all humans united as One as well as their separateness, and to see evil as a consequence of ignorance. These qualities are all threads in the fabric of virtue; virtue being the moral ground of integrated and thus spiritual being. The insight that divine providence is always working to create balance with the shadow generated by ignorance and the unconscious is fundamental, as is the desire and motivation to help this balance emerge whenever possible. Finally, understanding the role that suffering plays in the transformation of the infinite stream of beings evolving towards their source creates freedom and acceptance of the bound conditions of life on this plane. It is suffering that spurs us all into growth. When the garden is sunny, it needs no attention. It is the pain and shadow in this world that necessitate change. Accepting these truths as a whole is wisdom, which is the ultimate spiritual attribute.

The soul in the third coincides with Jung's idea of ultimate wholeness residing in the number four. The progression whereby the opposites (the two) become unified into one through the transcendent function makes the third or new level of being. This third level allows the fourth, or the One, Self and archetypal realm to be reflected into consciousness in the third, creating experience of the fourth or whole. In this manner the soul experiences dual-unity with God or the archetype of the Self (the fourth). The realization of God or the Self (the fourth) remains unattainable without the development of the third, which is why Jung called Christ the third son-ship. Christ as the whole man brought the divine light into human consciousness—this exemplifies the fourth within the third. The revelation of awareness in the third is a shift that is more profound and purposeful then a mere transition to a new conscious attitude, it is consciousness on another level, a window into the numinous and divine.

To summarize, consciousness transforms to another level through the transcendent function when energy is held back or suspended from expression of the opposites in the complex, which are then united within. Rather than experiencing opposites as coming to one's attention from without in unexpected personal events, opposites are felt internally and recognized as belonging to one's own self. Painful events continue to occur in life, but when one experiences the opposites coming together and being unified within, one's interpretation of reality shifts to a deeper more spiritual perception. When this occurs, the archetype at the center of every complex, and the Self at the center of every archetype, is individually felt through the aspect of unity in the dual-unity of the third.

Applying the will to suspend a complex in order to observe its contents has "an uncontrollable reactive effect on these same contents" (Jung 1969c, 229), and also one must take account of the "uncontrollable effects the observer has upon the system observed" (p. 229). Here Jung is referring to the subject-object (unconscious and conscious) nature of work in individuation and transformation, the fact that subjective attention (consciousness) upon objective processes (the unconscious) transforms both of these aspects. This transformation is unknown or mysterious, and therefore called an uncontrolled reaction.

Although the path of transformation is always mysterious and individual, it is also collective because incrementally the archetype, and the Self at the center of the archetype, emerge into awareness. Jung says the effect this emergence has on a person is a transformation because "the confrontation of the two [unconscious and conscious] positions generates a tension charged with energy and creates a living, third thing...a living birth that leads to a new level of being" (Jung 1969c, 90). As we have seen, this new level of being, that is the realm of the soul, has its own energy, form, intensity, and extensity, as described by Jung in canalization. Awareness in soul is a rebirth into a non-spatial and non-temporal reality that is not grossly physical, part of the brain, the biology of the body, or concrete in nature. When energy and thus consciousness moves from the old structures to the new, consciousness expands to include not only the physical body, the ego-related body, but also the higher soul with its own subtle body.

Uniting instinct and spirit, this transformation of consciousness into the subtle, energetic, immaterial matter of soul in the third is a rebirth creating the essential man (Jung 1966, 110), and fuels individual development (1971, 449). In describing different forms of rebirth in *The Archetypes and the Collective Unconscious,* Jung (1968a, 114) describes it as "the transformation...of a corporeal into a spiritual being" and the "raising up of the *corpus glorificationis*, the 'subtle body.'" (p. 114). I think we have seen that this new level of being is created in the transcendent function, is individual soul in a third ontological position, and that soul is in dual-unity with the divine Self, archetype and ego. The creation of consciousness in soul also signifies an energetic body of immaterial substance. Let's now go on to what Jung had to say about the subtle body of soul.

Psychoid Matter

The subtle body of soul is an immaterial substance. Validation for this immaterial substance can be found in quantum physics. Jung's idea of psychoid matter seems to have come out of his collaboration with quantum physicist Wolfgang Pauli. It is equated with the invisible, always in motion, atomic matter that Jung located on the ultraviolet end of the psychic spectrum. The archetype is psychoid, both in its living matter and its transcendent realm:

Regarding the *nature* of the archetype. The archetypal representation (images and ideas) mediated to us by the unconscious should not be confused with the archetype … The archetype as such is a psychoid factor that belongs, as it were, to the invisible, ultraviolet end of the psychic spectrum (Jung 1969c, 213).

In another passage, Jung identifies the archetype as psychoid: "The real nature of the archetype is not capable of being made conscious, that it is transcendent, on which account I call it psychoid" (1969c, 213). Because it is transcendent, it is psychoid, and the Self, which is the ultimate transcendent reality, must also be psychoid. Jung attested to his own experience of the transcendent Self or God, so he contradicts himself in this passage where he says the psychoid archetype cannot be made conscious. Like the psychoid Self, the psychoid archetype must also be felt or experienced consciously; certainly its image is a psychic experience, as Jung's *Red Book* is filled with such images. The numinous, holy quality of the archetype in individual experience is also transcendent and therefore psychoid.

The archetype, because it is psychoid energy matter, always remains psychoid. When it descends, it conforms to limitations that make it psychic because it is expressed through the complex, but it still retains its psychoid nature. Both psychoid and psychic, the archetype at the center of the complex can potentially reflect the psychoid consciousness of the archetypal realm and the Self, (or God) into psychic consciousness. Jung differentiates between psychoid and psychic when he states,

> The physicist does not believe that the transcendental reality represented by his psychic model is also psychic. He calls it matter, and in the same way the psychologist in no wise attributes a psychic nature to his images or archetypes. He calls them psychoids and is convinced that they represent transcendental realities. (Jung 1976, 683)

When the psychic complex unites in conscious soul with the psychoid archetype, the soul becomes aware of its psychic-psychoid dual-unity, and thus the transcendental nature of higher reality. Jung relates this knowing or awareness of the psychoid to the grace of God: it is a

> gift of the Holy Spirit. There is only one divine spirit—an immediate presence … surrender to God is a formidable adventure, and as "simple" as any situation over which man has no control. He who can risk himself wholly to it finds himself directly in the hands of God (1976, 683).

The Nature of Psychoid

The divine spirit (Self or God), the archetype, and the soul Jung distinguishes as psychoid because they exist in a spectrum of energy beyond our concrete and even our psychic world. Although Jung states that the psychoid is an adjective and not a noun (1976, 177), he also clearly identifies the psychoid archetype as a "living being" in another world, which would suggest the need to use a noun to identify it. The psychoid is "without psychic qualities except for a quasi-psychic one" (1969c, 177), pointing to the fact that it is distinguished from the psychic and instinctual: it is "a category of events [distinguished] from merely vitalistic phenomena on the one hand and from specifically psychic processes on the other" (p. 177). The psychoid suggests to Jung the reality of the unconscious possessing a subject—subject again implying a noun—and this subject would be "a second psychic system coexisting with consciousness—no matter what qualities we suspect it of possessing" (p. 178). This second system coexisting with conscious- ness is a "psychoid aura that "surrounds consciousness" (1970b, 551). Although the images translated into our psychic complex from the psychoid are variable and may be doubted, Jung emphasizes that "the existence of a transcendental reality is indeed evident in itself" (p. 551), regardless of our compromised intellectual efforts to understand it.

Jung locates both the psychic and psychoid together in the uncon- scious: "There is not only a psychic but also a psychoid unconscious" (p. 552). The complex of personal contents surrounding the archetype is the psychic unconscious. The archetype and its center, the Self/God, are the psychoid unconscious, which Jung also called the supercon- sciousness. When the transcendent function brings the archetype into felt experience through soul, psychic energy becomes consciously linked with the psychoid. Remembering the discussion on the transfer of energy from one form to another, the psychic complex transforming to psychoid matter means movement from a lower to a higher form. Therefore, something of the old structure, namely the complex, is carried into the third where it unites with the psychoid matter of the archetypal realm.

Jung (1970b, 551) describes the psychoid quality of the archetype as its inspiration, its transcendence (1970a, 453), and also its nature as the sphere of the *unus mundus*, equivalent to world soul in Plato. This is the unitary world upon which Jung felt the psychologist and atomic physicist were converging (p. 452). The psychoid archetype is un- conscious, parapsychological, synchronistic and nonlocal (p. 450-452). The last term Jung borrowed from physics, and refers to the archetype and psychoid matter simultaneously being in more than one place at a time (nonlocal). Jung specifies that psychoid is a descriptive term for functions whose existence we cannot know fully (1969c, 185), and that the archetype's psychic image originates in this transcendent, psychoid nature (1970b, 551), and retains this character at all stages of development (1967a, 272).

It is clear that the psychoid archetype goes beyond what Jung has attributed to the psychic realm. As mentioned earlier, it goes into "living matter" (Jung 1976, 257), which is "an unsolved mystery" (1971, 543). Jung refers to the whole psyche as equivalent to a living body of animated matter (p. 543). This unity of the psyche with a body of animated matter points to the psychoid nature of the soul's body as well as the underlying energy that sustains all life. Jung thinks about the relationship of physical matter to spiritual or energetic matter:

> Physics is pushing forward to insights which, if they do not exactly "de-materialize" matter, at least endue it with properties of its own… Matter therefore would contain the seed of spirit and spirit the seed of matter. …The "psychization" of matter puts the absolute immateriality of spirit in question since this would then have to be accorded a kind of substantiality. (1968a, 108-109)

Jung (1969c, 216) goes on in *The Structure and Dynamics of the Psyche,* describing the psychoid nature of the archetype as a "bridge to matter in general." It seems Jung is suggesting that the immaterial matter of the psychoid realm connects to denser matter in the physical world because of the hypostasis of energy. Whether considering the archetype or physical reality, Jung says, "Matter and spirit both appear in the psychic realm as distinctive qualities of conscious contents" (p. 216). Psychoid matter is spirit and appears in consciousness because all psychic reality is energetic in nature.

The contents of our minds, both the conscious and unconscious, because they are energetic, exist on their own in the psychoid realm and appear as symbols and instinct in the psychic sphere. Since these contents are invisible until manifested in actions in the outer world, their reality is subtle and immaterial rather than gross and material. Jung reasons in *Two Essays* that "spirit is a psychic fact" (1966, 185), and that very early on, humankind discovered the "concrete existence of a spirit-world" (p. 185). These thoughts, put together with Jung's later speculations about psychoid matter, describe an energetic substance that exists on a subtle level we cannot perceive with our five physical senses.

Jung explains that this psychoid substance of the spirit world is the source of psychosis, when a person loses their relationship with consensual reality. The psychoid, archetypal world takes precedence over sensory data in this case: "Spirits are complexes of the collective unconscious which appear when the individual loses his adaptation to reality" (1969c, 315). This concept of psychosis as an unintegrated bleeding through into consciousness of another dimension of reality fits with Jung's belief that "the dead are not in a different place from the living. There is only a difference in their 'frequencies'" (1976, 315). Jung's reference to different vibrational frequencies explains a reality or dimension that normal human consciousness cannot perceive.

Energetic Realms

The reality of frequencies is a scientific fact that helped Jung develop his ideas of the psychoid world. The idea of a frequency functioning as a boundary that delineates one realm from another introduces a possible threshold between the physical and psychic, and psychic and psychoid. It is here that experience changes from one level of perception to another. Jung points to the fact that sound and light frequencies have a spectrum beyond the threshold of the human senses. This convinces him that the same kind of spectrum can be applied to the psyche, supporting or validating the existence of psychoid matter. In terms of transformation, it is "the very peculiar effect the psyche has upon matter" (1976, 314) that makes unconscious contents psychically conscious—a reference to matter as an immaterial substance crossing a threshold of consciousness in individuation. Jung's considerations about frequencies lead him to believe in the "energic conception of the psyche" (p. 314) something that goes beyond spiritualism since validated by his own psychological findings.

Putting attention upon one's own conscious and unconscious mind in individuation creates consciousness on another level, a level in which one can observe one's ego process as well as experience a spiritual, psychoid state that exists outside space and time. Space and time, central to Jung's theory of synchronicity, are psychic discriminations that do not impact the frequency of the psychoid. Space and time, Jung reminds us, are "properties of bodies in motion … their relativization by psychic conditions … presents itself when the psyche observes, not external bodies, but *itself*" (Jung 1969c, 436). Observing itself, the psyche somehow transforms the properties of bodies as well as unconscious contents.

Since bodies are relative to space and time, Jung concludes they must have a certain psychoid property (1969c, 505). Synchronicity, which is a causeless order or harmony that also appears to include absolute knowledge (p. 506) is transcendental, so it is also related to psychoid matter. The equivalence of the transcendental and psychoid may "clear up the body-soul problem" (p. 506) by defining the body as not only physical, but also as having a subtle, psychoid form. All the levels of energy unite in consciousness of soul.

The degree to which the physical, psychic, and psychoid dimensions are unified within human awareness conditions a person's level of consciousness. This is a cyclical, transformational process. A person who is working to individuate eventually quiets the storm of opposition in the ego. Such a person is less caught up by conflicted patterns and habits of mind that keep the ego very busy and is able to observe the complex and its action while living through their immediate experience.

Attention is less drawn to the complex because the internal mind of the ego has been to some degree transcended and experience in soul is more unified, harmonized and peaceful. Each advance in this process brings a new degree of awareness in soul, which is a purity or "polish" of consciousness that is mirrored in the ego thus allowing the reflective function of dual-unity its full play in experience. In this way the cycle returns, bringing ever higher degrees of psychoid, psychic and physical unity into consciousness reflected in the ego.

Remembering that matter is hypostasized in Plato into descending levels of being from the One, Jung follows closely when he remarks in *The Structure and Dynamics of the Psyche,* "energy immediately hypostatizes itself" (1969c, 30). Here he refers to the energy of libido, which is energetic and therefore points to processes of transformation rather than mechanistic causality (p. 31). To hypostatize means to symbolize in material form, meaning that each level of energetic hypostasis is a material symbol of the higher, previous, level of being. Each level symbolizes the higher level, representing that which cannot be manifested on a lower level. Formally considered, the nature of the individual self and the Self in Jungian psychology consists of derivations of energetically hypostatized matter. These derivations descend in order from the Self or God, to psychoid matter in the soul and in the archetypal realm, to psychic soul in the functional complex that becomes psychoid when developed, to the psychic complexes, and then finally the physical matter of body. Each level, including the physical, is made more conscious upon an individual's psychological transformation and spiritual ascent.

All this psychological transformation results in transformation of substances. Jung has described the transformation of substances as an energetic fact in development. These changes happen in the transcendent function and unify the descending energies. Jung says,

> The idea of development requires the possibility of change in substances, which, from the energetic standpoint, appear as systems

of energy capable of theoretically unlimited interchangeability and modulation. … From the energetic standpoint … substance is nothing more than the expression or sign of an energetic system. (Jung 1969c, 22)

Jung embraces human development as a result of the transformation and exchange of energetic substances within and between systems— physical, psychic, psychoid. Furthermore, emotion generated in physical nature reflects "the heavy matter of the body" (Jung 1976, 138). Whether one crawls along the slow road of the natural gradient in growth or accelerates awareness through individuation, it seems the unifying of the opposites within the complexes and the resolution of ego-based emotional conflict transform the heavy matter of the body into psychoid matter, which has growing degrees of freedom from the lower systems. Development occurs naturally or with intention. When one engages intentionally in the process of individuation, one purposely creates awareness of ever-finer degrees of energy and. therefore enjoys ever-finer degrees of consciousness spanning the continuum from physical to psychoid. This eventually yields one whole substance. This arrangement reflects an ancient model of the human being that is compatible with phenomenon at the quantum level where all life is One, and the invisible and visible worlds coincide. In Jungian terms, the Self gives forth the living matter of the psychoid archetype and soul, which connects to the psychic world manifested in the physical organism. Jung describes the cascade or hypostasis of creation where the higher level is in dual-unity with the lower in comments like this one: "Living matter has a psychic aspect, and the psyche a physical aspect" (1970a, 411). Thus, all the worlds rest within the psychoid Self, and Jung considers the ramifications when he comments that perhaps all reality is "grounded on an as yet unknown substrate possessing material and at the same time psychic qualities…afford[ing] us the opportunity to construct a new world model closer to the idea of the *unus mundus* (p. 411).

The *unus mundus* or one world is a Platonic doctrine, where the whole cosmos is at its heart one divine, transcendent substance that transforms to encompass many degrees of matter from the densest physical to the most refined or psychoid light. All these substances reflect levels of consciousness, degrees of energy that originate in light and descend into other forms. Modern atomic science defines light as photons, invisible packets that are always in motion yet when taken together constitute the seamless fabric of space-time. The ancient Platonic wisdom defined light as a divine being. Both of these perspectives are the ground or foundation of gross, consensual reality. The human subject can comprehend this light however it is defined because it is already within the individual self. It is "akin to him and is wrought of his own psychic substance" (Jung 1976, 667). The power of cosmic or archetypal light to create life is evident, but the power of that same light within the human psyche is yet to be appreciated, and scientifically verified. It is this light, mirrored in the soul, that is the healing agent in psychotherapy.

The transcendent light can only be experienced, like any other mystical reality—it is incomprehensible from an intellectual or concrete vantage point. It is an issue of feeling energetic values. Jung hypothesizes that "psychic processes stand in some sort of energy relation to the physiologic substrate. In so far as they are objective events, they can hardly be interpreted as anything but energy processes" (1969c, 233). Although Jung footnotes his query about whether the whole psyche could be energetic, in other places he has reasoned that psychoid energy is the subatomic energy of the quantum world and the ground of all being. He also reasons that the subtle, psychoid body must exist when he equates the qualitative in physics, and the quantitative or intensity factor in psychology:

> The psychic intensities and their graduated differences point to quantitative processes which are inaccessible to direct observation and measurement .... Could these quantities be measured the

psyche would be bound to appear as having motion in space, something to which the energy formula would be applicable. Therefore, since mass and energy are of the same nature, mass and velocity would be adequate concepts for characterizing the psyche so far as it has any observable effects in space: in other words, it must have an aspect under which it would appear as mass in motion … A postulate not so very far removed from certain formulations of modern physics. (1969c, 234)

Jung's speculations, and even further, his belief in and experience of psychoid, subatomic matter, and the body having a subtle psychoid reality lead him to remark, "If these reflections are justified, they must have weighty consequences with regard to the nature of the psyche" (p. 234).

In *The Archetypes and the Collective Unconscious,* Jung declares his conclusions about the consequences when he describes the nature of the psyche as an immaterial psychoid substance, or a spirit with a subtle body:

A connection between spirit and physical conditions is not immediately apparent, and for this reason it [spirit] was credited with immateriality to a much higher degree than was the case with psychic phenomena in the narrower sense. Not only is a certain physical dependence attributed to the latter, but they are themselves [psychic phenomena] thought of as possessing a kind of materiality, as the idea of the subtle body…we cannot very well accept the total immateriality of the psyche. (1968a, 212)

Jung acknowledges that since it is not apparent, there is difficulty in accepting the subtle body as an entity that is spiritual, includes psychic phenomenon, connects the physical and spiritual worlds, and also supports a dependent physicality. As our ideas of matter have changed so radically in the twentieth century, he predicts that as science pushes forward there will be evidence to support the fact of subtle matter and being. He says,

It is, however, not easy to see why our hypothetical "matter," which looks quite different from what it did even thirty years ago, alone should be real and spirit not … Spirit and matter may well be forms of one and the same transcendental being. (1968a, 212)

For Jung, becoming an individual soul awake in the transcendental realm in relation to God—a soul awake in the third, the realm of subtle, psychoid energy—is God's work. He says, "Christ is the model for the human answers and his symbol is the cross, the union of the opposites" (1976, 735). It is only when the opposites have been separated in order to come together again that the individual can "take up a middle position and discover a middle way. That is the task left to man, and that is the reason why man is so important to God that he decided to become a man himself" (p. 735). Jung (1968b, 283) says the middle way or the position of realization is neither mind nor matter but "that intermediate realm of subtle reality." Summarizing the intermediate realm in reference to alchemical work, Jung claims

The moment when physics touches on the "untrodden, untreadable regions," and when psychology has to admit that there are other forms of psychic life … when psychology too touches on impenetrable darkness—then the intermediate realm of subtle bodies comes to life again, and the physical and psychic are once more blended in an indissoluble unity. We have come very near to this turning point today. (1968b, 279)

Jung's work on the psychoid as an energetic form of spiritualized matter is the turning point in his theory of self where self, soul, and subtle body come together. Let's go on to Jung's own work on what the subtle body is in history, culture, and his own clinical work.

The Subtle Body

Jung's work on the psychology of psychoid matter, its role in the archetype and transcendent sphere and thus the human soul, shows us the depth of his considerations around the existence of subtle, energetic matter bridging the ontological gap between realms or levels of reality. This body of work leads naturally into Jung's explorations into the existence of a subtle body in his clinical work and in the history of philosophy and religion.

Zarathustra

I found Jung's philosophical and religious investigations of the subtle body in his seminars on Nietzsche's Zarathustra. They were completed in 1939, twenty years before Jung wrote his final version of the essay on the transcendent function. In these seminars, the discussions he facilitated about the nature of the subtle body seem to have contributed to his later conclusion that psychoid matter, or immaterial transcendent substance, exists as the primary nature of transcendent realms and as a cohesive background factor within the psyche.

Zarathustra emerges as a subtle, divine or semi-divine aspect of Nietzsche's psyche, "A river of psychical material personified" (Jung 1988b, 1486) that comes into awareness through Nietzsche's involvement in Hermeticism, an esoteric philosophy that aims at spiritual development. Zarathustra, Jung says, through "the opus of Hermetic philosophy…[is] a sort of subtle body" (p. 1486), which he identifies with the Self. Jung equivocates or is typically unclear here how the Self could be commensurate with a subtle body, and he juxtaposes the totality of divine being with its human counterpart without defining the individual clearly enough. However, this juxtaposition gets clearer as he identifies this subtle body with Christ, who is a union of the divine and human. As I have discussed elsewhere, Christ represents the epitome of the developed soul and not the Self. Zarathustra is "like Christ himself, a Christ that comes after Christ, a new savior" (p. 1486). This subtle figure of Zarathustra is more developed than Nietzsche's ego self, in fact, Zarathustra is "greater than any light in the world" (p. 1486). Jung says that Zarathustra is "a transformation of something low into something that is valuable" (p. 1486), it is the ordinary personality raised up into the transcendent realm.

Zarathustra is the higher, more valuable self in relation to the lower personality. In the psychology of the soul in the third and its dual-unity with other aspects or levels of the psyche, Zarathustra would be identified with the soul because it is the soul that is "Christ-like," thus able to transmit the divine Self or God into experience. Similar inspiration was transmitted to Jung through the personification of his own transcendent self, Philemon, a figure readers may be familiar with. Both Philemon and Zarathustra carry the spiritual or transcendent "fourth" dimension of the divine into the third son-ship or soul; leading each to a unique path of individuation. Zarathustra and Philemon symbolize the Christ or savior by receiving inspiration from the creative source of being, therefore completing the lower self. As I have said before, for Jung, Christ consciousness represented the ultimate goal for human growth, that is, the whole man.

During the seminar, Nietzsche's Zarathustra was likened to a bird that was not only a messenger, but also established itself permanently by building a "nest" within. This nest of the soul represented a world outside time that hatches the "golden eggs" or the highest spiritual value within the psyche. The "bird" as a spiritual symbol of Zarathustra is not a conflict between body and spirit, but "a body that *is* (my italics) a spiritual body" (Jung 1988a, 431). Zarathustra as spiritual body unifies and therefore solves the conflicts between higher and lower. It is "that middle thing which the primitives call 'the subtle body'… It is the union of the two [physical body and spiritual self] by this thing between" (p. 432).

Jung explains that the subtle body of soul is an old idea. He finds anthropological evidence for it in his own experience of the psychology and religion of primitive people living in Africa, where it is represented by a bird or smoke rising out of the coarse body and floating free. In another more ancient Mesopotamian myth, the Epic of Gilgamesh, the bird is also the symbol of the soul who sinks into the sad places of Hades. In Egypt the bird symbolizes divinity when the king puts feathers on, appearing in plumage in order to symbolize the transformation of the soul. Transformation into a bird after death according to Jung "refers to the lightness of the subtle body" (1988a, 186). Further discussion ensues concerning eating and fasting in ascetic forms of religion as a way of attaining spirituality. Zarathustra attempts to protect himself and preserve his subtlety by avoiding the vulgarity of eating, which brings him into the heaviness of the common and ordinary.

Eating fetters the individual to the earth because the subtle body becomes heavy and weighted down by earthly food. Food that sustains higher or soul consciousness must be metaphysical, enabling the body to lift itself up and even levitate and fly. Wise men in India are able to fly because they have attained the state of Hamsa, a state of wisdom, lightness, and subtlety that is symbolized by the swan (1988a, 186). Saints who have survived by eating only the host are examples of beings that are spiritualized to the point of being able to "rise" and transcend the lower spheres. Flying, a state of spiritualization reached only by wise men, is attained by Zarathustra when he goes down into the under-world.

Jung relates the winged lightness of the subtle body to the Holy Grail, a symbol for a state of consciousness held in suspension, which precedes birth or creation. Jung says, "The Holy Grail itself is held in a state of suspension… by angels suspended between heaven and earth" (Jung 1988a, 187). The state of suspension is related to crucifixion, the unconscious aspect of transfiguration. He goes on to explain,

Suspension is also an aspect of crucifixion, the unconscious aspect of transfiguration. It is the state of transformation, but it is the fate of the body while transfiguration is the fate of the subtle body... That tormented state of suspension is the incubation of the subtle body." (p. 187)

This reference to suspension, which Jung later applied to his transcendent function, refers to Christ's transformation from the physical body to the subtle, through the crucifixion. The Holy Grail, which is a vessel for the sacred, is a symbol of transformation, i.e., the body with its subtle soul-body within. Christ, his body hanging on the cross between the opposites of heaven and earth or the divine and sense worlds, survives physical death in his subtle body of soul. Jung reminds us that "Christ was seen after his crucifixion by his disciples and by many other people; his subtle body appeared after the state of suspension" (Jung 1988a, 187). In Jungian terms, the cross is the symbol of individuation and crucifixion the state of suspension in the transcendent function that transforms the lower and produces the higher. Christ was transformed on the cross, sacrificing the physical body in order to give birth to the spiritual flesh—akin to the superman in Zarathustra.

As the symbol of the whole man as well as the prototype for human transformation, Christ's suspension on the cross and his death and transfiguration, shows humanity the path to real life, the life of the spirit. As is well known, Christ's visible resurrection into the subtle body eventually touched and inspired the world, and it is a wisdom teaching that Jung has intentionally carried forward.

The Union of Physical and Spiritual

Jung calls the subtle body a "very big problem in itself" (Jung 1988a, 441) in lecture VIII on March 13, 1935, and he also says that "very little is known about this strange concept." (p. 441). He references Mead's book on the topic and asks that a comprehensive report be made for the following term about this "body of breath" (p. 441), which he equates with the subtle body. Jung describes how the shadow as the psychological unconscious is understandable, but the subtle body as part of the unconscious is more difficult to grasp. "The part of the unconscious which is designated as the subtle body becomes more and more identical with the functioning of the body, and therefore it grows darker and darker and ends in the utter darkness of matter" (p. 441). As the subtle body approaches the boundary with the physical body it is encompassed in the utter darkness of physical matter, and eventually becomes identical with it. Ultimately this union with the physical sense-based body makes the subtle body just as unconscious as it was in its original state. The subtle body is difficult to perceive at either end of the spectrum. He points out that

> the physiological unconscious, the so-called somatic unconscious which is the subtle body.... becomes material, because the body is the living unit, and our conscious and our unconscious are embedded in it, they contact the body. Somewhere there is a place where the two ends meet and become interlocked. (p. 441)

The subtle and physical meet and become interlocked creating an entire spectrum of living matter from the subtlest to the grossest physical matter. As described earlier, Jung identified the spectrum of matter or energy as red on the physical end, and violet on the spiritual or subtle. Somewhere in the middle in-between the red and violet, the physical and subtle meet. Jung goes on to explore this in-between point in the Old Gnostic system.

Gnosticism identifies the pneuma as spirit above and the hyle (matter) or sarx (flesh) as the body below, which Paul referred to in the New Testament. In the middle is the sphere of the subtle body. In the Gnostic sect called Docetism, the Pistis Sophia—who is the female aspect of God, the goddess of wisdom and an archetypal being—incarnates as Jesus' birth mother Mary. Christ incarnates into the physical body of Jesus at the moment he was baptized by John and exits Jesus' body before the suffering of the crucifixion. After Jesus' death on the cross Christ shows himself to the disciples in his perfectly developed subtle body. These views competed with the centralized orthodox canon.

There were various important forces that produced what I am referring to as the orthodox canon, meaning the central, agreed upon doctrine of the early church. One of those forces was the ruthless and barbaric Roman persecution of the early Christians. Such a dangerous political climate brought a few powerful men together to create an organized form for the Christian religion. Their perspective was that safety for the struggling early church equaled control of this same church, so they decided what was true about Jesus, his teaching and his life. This group, through councils called for this purpose, declared the many other extant narratives about Jesus as corrupt and therefore heretical. The result of these activities was that important esoteric truths about Christianity were expunged from Christian life and only the outer form, which became dogma, was accepted.

Furthermore, spiritual development or experience was mediated through approved and appointed figures of the church according to these accepted exoteric or outer rituals and forms. As time went by, efforts to maintain control of the church translated into active persecution of those who refused to accept the centralized doctrine. Eventually these more esoteric or inner splinter schools were wiped out and therefore any overt discussion about Christ's subtle body was quashed.

Jung explains in the seminar that the idea of the subtle body exists not only in the Gnostic system but in the orthodox canon as well:

All these ideas of the subtle body play a great role in the New Testament. The body, or sarx, to St. Paul, is the gross, biological,

177

physiological body, the corruptible body; but he speaks also of the incorruptible body we put on with Christ, because Christ in a way is the soul or the pneuma, the incorruptible body that is beyond space or time. (Jung 1988a, 442)

He goes on to say if we accept the truth of the subtle body then it follows that

Every real body fills space because it consists of matter, while the subtle body is said not to consist of matter, or it is matter which is so exceedingly subtle that it cannot be perceived. So it must be a body which does not fill space, a matter which is beyond space and therefore it would be in no time…. this idea of the subtle body is very important. (Jung 1988a, 443)

Ultimately, Jung concludes in this discussion that the subtle body is not only important but a transcendent idea that cannot be grasped in language or philosophy because it exists outside the usual categories of reality, i.e., time and space.

In spite of this hardship, Jung goes on in his investigations of this elusive, transcendent state of being by looking across cultures and considering whether the subtle body is the diamond body of Chinese Yoga. The diamond body is an everlasting body produced through the practice of Yoga. Jung draws many parallels between Chinese Yoga and alchemy, concluding that both methods produce a body of the highest value from the vulgar or common body. This body of subtle substance, equivalent to the substance of the Self is

something with the qualities of light…located in the center-the psyche- between body and spirit—and consists of both. So in that respect one can say the concept of the diamond body is really identical with the idea of the subtle body. (Jung 1988a, 445)

In this quote Jung locates the psyche in the third between body and spirit. Speaking clearly of the subtle body, Jung explains that it starts as a primitive body and is transformed into the diamond body in conscious unity with the divine Self. Jung identifies the diamond body with the Self (1988a, 444) because at this final stage, the perfect body of light has been realized and the subtle body and the Self or God are all One and the same substance.

The subtle body in the center between the spiritual divine and physical body separates the somatic unconscious from the spiritual unconscious. This discussion seems to suggest that Jung understood a boundary or middle ground where the somatic unconscious or unconscious aspect of the physical body connects with the spiritual unconscious or archetypal world of the soul and Self. The diamond body emerges in the center or middle and is a condition where consciousness connects one dimension with another, body, soul and Self. Jung likens Chinese Yoga to alchemy, believing that alchemy should be called "the yoga process" (p. 445) because yoga is known for its focus on creating something of very great spiritual value within human experience.

Jung responds to another question about the subtle body being the source of all possibility in life by saying, that it is the Self rather than soul that arbitrates our lives, and that it exists in the middle between the spiritual and physical: "The self includes the somatic as well as the spiritual unconscious, being neither the one nor the other, but in between, in the psyche" (1988a, 449). In Jung's cosmology the Self is within all aspects of the psyche, so Jung's repeated contradictions of the middle or third representing the Self or soul seem to originate in his need to sometimes highlight the essential Self and at other times the soul. Since we have seen that the Self exits in dual-unity with soul, speaking of one implies the other, therefore, the conflict can be understood and resolved.

In the seminar, questions about the subtle body being the source of life continue with a woman wondering if the subtle body causes the physical. She experiences

the inside body [subtle body] as a free power, wherein all possibilities for forming or producing are given from one central point, which leads all events and reactions. [and asks] So is the putting of the body into life as the consequence to an inside demand, the subtle body? (1988a, 449)

After refuting her idea that the subtle body is the symbol for individuation, Jung responds to this question about the inner, subtle body creating the outer body. He develops this question by bringing in the metaphor of the building up of a crystal:

Well, from the standpoint of Platonic philosophy, the body is built up on the *eidos*, the eternal image of the human body. The human body would then be explained exactly as the making of a crystal is explained, by a sort of preexisting abstract axial system into which matter is filled. (1988a, 449)

Jung associates the Platonic eidos, the structure of the crystal, and a theory about the subtle body proposed by a Dr. Geley, who was a former director of the Institut de Metapsychologie in Paris. Geley viewed physiology from the standpoint of the subtle body and uses the "thoroughly Platonic idea" (1988a, 450) that "the subtle body directs and builds up the physical body" (p. 450). Although Jung says this theory is "very much against our hitherto valid physiological ideas," (p. 450) he emphasizes that from a scientific viewpoint there is as little proof on the one side as on the other (science or philosophy) and he embraces the possibility rather than refuting it. Ultimately, Jung asserts that since all phenomena manifest in opposites, we will always need both points of view in order to understand the whole (p. 450).

The question of the subtle body appears again in Jung's investigations into alchemy. Initially, the alchemical project involved the chemical oxidation of metals, which when heated up became volatile. The practical chemistry of changing a solid to a vapor eventually became a transformation or sublimation of one kind of being to a different being. The new being was a new body or spiritual body. Although the alchemists used the term spirit indiscriminately, even in their own texts, Jung says

> presumably they meant that the spirit is what the bible calls spirit— a subtle body. You don't get away from that; it is just a subtle body. So you can make a spirit out of matter, can de-materalize—-what they call subtilize matter to such an extent that it becomes a spirit, not a disembodied spirit but a spirit that is a subtle body. (1988b, 1067)

The alchemist's assertion that "thou hast not accomplished the work if thou dost not succeed in making the body a spirit" (Jung 1988b, 1067), implies that the methods aimed at more than the application of heat to mercury and its condensation into a higher part of the vessel. The oxidation of mercury into a "spirit" or vapor referred to the effect of fire on the substance of the body, fire being a symbol of trans- formation and the soul (p. 1067). Applying fire or heat to substances created subtle bodies by the eradication of their impurities. Jung quotes Mathew 3:11 to illustrate how Christ will baptize with fire, and that he is fire itself. The fire of Christ represents the greatest possible intensity of being, and those who have contact with this fire are subtilized. Christ refers to this in the non-canonical saying "He who is near to me is near to the fire; and he who is far from me is far from the kingdom" (p. 1068). The fire is a power that can destroy or transform, and the alchemical opus has succeeded when the heavy body is made into a pneumatic or a volatile, subtle body.

Jung develops this alchemical theme in his work on the transcendent function where the intensity of consciously holding the opposites together in suspension without allowing one-sided expression transforms or canalizes consciousness into a subtler form—soul in the "third" —conscious of the fire or the divine light of psychoid (subtilized) matter. As we have seen in the earlier section on psychoid matter, the idea of subtilized matter becomes part of Jung's theoretical equipment when he asserts that there is a subtilized, immaterial, spiritual matter underlying all form in the universe. The psychoid archetype is a whole realm or world supporting the physical reality we perceive through our senses.

Jung presents some clinical cases as either suggestive of a subtle body experience or directly involving subtle body experience. One of the areas Jung considered was evidence of psychic processes occurring during unconscious states. For example, a sensation of levitation or rising up from the physical body in men who had been wounded in battle, and in a case of head injury where a person experienced levitation in a body that was weightless. A mood of euphoria described as "buoyant, solemn, heavenly, serene, relaxed, blissful, expectant, exciting" accompanies these experiences (Jung 1969c, 507).

Cases of deep coma also produce this experience. Jung presents a woman who had a complicated childbirth after a long labor. While unconscious the subject experienced a separation from the body and was able to witness the behavior of the doctor and nurse as well as conversations and acts performed by her family. She was aware of an entrance into another world, a beautiful landscape where she had perception independent of space or time. She knew she could leave this world if she would but pass through into the forest, but knew she was not going (Jung 1969c, 508). She reported what had happened with the professional helpers, which matched the actual reality. Jung marvels that this woman "really was in a coma" and ought to have been incapable of any perception and comprehension. Instead of a black out the patient was observing all events, and complex psychic processes were occurring within her from where she hovered, somewhere above her physical body.

In *Two Essays* (1966), Jung reports working with another patient who had powerful visions through the practice of active imagination connected with her individuation journey. Through the transcendent function she joined the conscious and the unconscious, and reached a mid-point through the union of opposites. He describes the symbolism of her vision, which involved four statues and a circle of fire into which flame she transcended. Becoming part of the flame within her vision she had an ascension experience that Jung explains as "the genesis of the 'subtle spirit'" (1966, 223). This genesis of the subtle spirit is a transformation of the personality into a whole and a state of exaltation. This transformation of the personality into the subtle state that indicates wholeness depends on the transcendent function and does not indicate a total absorption into the divine. Jung sums this up simply when he says, "The way of the transcendent function is an individual destiny" (p. 224).

The transcendent function and individual destiny shape the path of individuation, a teleological journey that actualizes consciousness of the personality into soul. Individuation is deeply affected by what Jung calls the Spirit of the Age (1969, 340), because the Spirit of the Age bends individual thought to the socially acceptable norms. In this vein, Jung asserts that the norm current in his day (which is still present today) maintained the exclusive reality of physical, concrete matter. This collective social perception resulted and still results in a belief that soul or psyche is an epiphenomenon of the brain. Such a one-sided commitment is a natural enantiodromia, a reaction from histories earlier preoccupation with the religious point of view. Such a powerful reversal of perspective would be "ludicrous" (p. 340), Jung remarks, if it weren't so clearly connected with the inevitable swing in the collective unconscious process, which moves between the opposites.

While admitting that the current intellectual climate refutes the substantiality of the psyche, Jung wishes we were more able to make use of history, understand the inevitable swings between the opposites, and thus learn to be more critical of our fundamental assumptions. Instead of expressing only one side of the opposition between body and spirit in our Zeitgeist we as a culture should follow the path of wholeness, and therefore accept both sides of the dilemma. If we were able to do so, the reality of the spirit, which has been consigned to the shadow for 200 years or more, would be consciously in balance with our attitude of value towards the physical. Knowledge about visible reality would be matched by an equal commitment to the invisible, and Jung's beautiful summation of our historical insight into the nature of that invisible self could be accepted today as he declares it here:

> *Man* has a soul; that soul has substance, is of divine nature and therefore immortal; that there is a power inherent within it which builds up the body, sustains its life, heals its ills and enables the soul to live independently of the body. (Jung 1969c, 341)

The Platonic Philosophical Life and Jungian Individuation

Plato and Jung present similar systems for spiritual and psychological growth. The primary aim of both systems is to produce teleological return to our spiritual origin through awareness of soul. One system, called individuation, is commonly nurtured in a consulting room in the presence of a therapist; the other, called philosophy, was nurtured in the academy in relationship to a teacher. Individuation in the context of therapy includes emotional processes involving interpretation and other therapeutic acts that have not been recorded as part of Plato's climb to the divine, but since Plato's teaching was mostly an oral tradition, much of it has not been recorded (noted in a personal conversation with Tim Addey). It seems safe to assume that the philosophy masters provided important or even crucial emotional experiences for their students. Both systems have the same goal, to lead the pilgrim through the transformation from sensible man or ego-oriented man to a person possessed of an individual soul consciously able to mirror divine life.

The capacity to mirror divine life is an experience that is also a form of knowledge. Such knowledge is mystical rather than rational. It cannot be fully explained or described although there are those who have helped us understand, and one can look to the history of mysticism to find these special people, including Plato and Jung. These two great men have taught us that the level of being required for mystical knowledge is a unity of macrocosm and microcosm, the whole with the part. The sense of self and world that accompany this unity change the intrinsic striving inherent in the sensible and ego-oriented person. External values continue to have meaning but a person who has walked far enough along this path becomes more and more focused on inner depth, and the original source of the human spirit.

Attainment of these experiences is an essential condition for the postmortem life in Plato, and Jung said he was "in agreement…with Plato, who regarded philosophy as a preparation for death" (Jung 1976, 315). Jung's attitude about human development was that the first half of life was meant to be devoted towards mastering the outer situation, for example having a family and investing in a career, while the second half of life was meant for inner exploration in preparation for death. Although individuation in analytic therapy is useful at any time in life, it is especially effective in the second half of life.

Personal development through philosophy and individuation begins with conflict and turbulence and involves sacrifice. Plato speaks of the sacrifice as purification and separation of lower from higher that leads to freedom from the irrational and spirited appetites and the rule of the body. Similarly, Jung felt that the opposites had to be separated in bodily consciousness in order to be experienced. Then, through suspending the will (separating) from identification with the (conflicted, turbulent) opposites, one transcends them and the mind is purified and freed from their power. This is a sacrifice for the ego whose life is fed and sustained by the identification with these opposites that comprise the complexes. The potential of transcending these identifications is man's legacy from God.

For Jung, Christ was the ultimate symbol of God's legacy to man. His life and death illustrated for all people the potential for reaching a unified consciousness of our divine source, as well as the recognition that the subtle, spiritual flesh exists after the death of the body. Jung took a stand on the relationship between the individual and God when he said, "Christ…either lost his wholeness or gave it away to mankind and can only get it back again through man's integration. His wholeness depends on man" (Jung 1969b, 293). A person's choice to integrate the opposites and sacrifice the primacy of the ego is a conscious act of reciprocation for the gift of life. It creates God's wholeness as well as our own because as a part of God, if we are not whole, somehow neither is God. Sacrifice of the ego's primacy is only an apparent loss. The soul when awakened experiences the whole, with each aspect of the psyche in balance.

Jung's idea of sacrifice in terms of suspending oneself from the opposites in a complex (therefore dis-identifying with the ego experience of the complex) is very similar to Plato's purification. The aim of both is "to detach consciousness from the object so the individual no longer places the guarantee of his happiness or of his life even, in factors outside himself" (Jung 1976, 166). As philosophy proceeds, a person realizes that happiness and life itself are anchored to images and forms within, rather than sense-based objects or experiences without.

For Jung, detaching from one side or the other in any conflict generated by complexes means that either part of the conflict would no longer be projected outside oneself. Instead it will be re-collected, unified with its opposite, and experienced within. Perception and identity change in this act. Jung describes giving up one's historical and acquired complex psychology as a "sacrifice, [achieved] by renouncing the personal tie to childhood" (1967b, 420). He also refers to individuation as "a work of patience, self-sacrifice, and devotion" (1968a, 241). I think Plato would agree with the latter description, but not the comment about sacrificing ties to childhood. Modern psychology has addressed the childhood origins of habits and appetites. This may have been part of the oral teaching of philosophy in Plato's times but the Dialogues are silent on this.

The suffering involved in transcending the ego or the sensible man according to both Jung and Plato is central to developing consciousness in soul. Jung says that transcendence "involves suffering, a passion of the ego" (Jung 1969b, 157). Likewise, in Plato, mastery or rational control over the passions or appetitive and spirited man means the painstaking work of giving up the attitudes and habits of a familiar life. Plato and Jung both suggest that by sacrificing the lower through this work on the self, one gains the immeasurable glories of the higher, and that gaining these glories is a religious enlightenment. Jung called individuation a *via sancta*, a highway that is a Holy Way (1968a, 350n).

While on the Holy Way of philosophy and individuation, the ability to experience the intelligible world and the One, or the Self and archetypes, changes the very nature of suffering. Suffering is no longer defined as happening entirely in the conflict of opposites and awareness has entered to some degree into four levels of being, ego (sensible man), soul, and the archetypal (intelligible) realm and the One or Self within it. On the Holy Way a person suffers while simultaneously experiencing a degree of freedom from that same suffering. Suffering experienced with access to the soul becomes more objective because an archetypal perspective includes knowledge of spiritual realities and therefore conducts a universal and eternal perspective into perception and understanding.

Suffering only within the ego, without this higher perspective, is an experience without the mitigating comfort or buffer of the spiritual world, so it can present any degree of torment. The almost limitless ways the small self can suffer temporal losses in the ego's sphere can be overwhelming and is inherent in life on this plane of dualities. Receiving support from transcendent sources happens when soul has developed the capacity to look into the depth of being. Spiritual reality provides comfort and direction for our here and now world if we are able to reach it. Ordinary suffering cannot be avoided but it can be transformed if there is a commitment to developing soul. Help is available from the spiritual world but the relationship with the spiritual must be cultivated in order to achieve knowledge and experience.

Achieving a higher level of being in soul adds the resource of compassionate love and understanding—qualities that are mirrored from divine being that also transform suffering arising in the ego. Sorrow in company with these spiritual attributes can transform the aspects of suffering that stem from reactions involving hate, revenge, bitterness, rage, persecution, and so forth. The higher the capacity for love, the more an individual is able to master the self-absorbed preoccupation with feeling victimized by others or circumstances. From the higher perspective, pain is understood as unavoidable in this world and accepted as necessary to either spur growth or contribute to conditions that remain a mystery—not so easy to see from our usual standpoint. Compassionate love, coupled with understanding, are components of wisdom, a divine attribute for both Plato and Jung.

During individuation, one transforms suffering produced through the unintegrated shadow complex by becoming conscious of denied aspects of the personality and then relating adequately to them. Mirroring Plato's idea of rational mastery Jung's individuation aims to "set up a rational, spiritual-psychic position over against the turbulence of the emotions" (Jung 1970b, 489), and to "establish a spiritual position which is supraordinate to the turbulent sphere of the body" (p. 471). In Plato's philosophy mastery occurs by the rational soul gaining a position over and against the turbulent and passionate emotions of the spirited psyche and the ordinary appetites of the body. With Plato, false virtues practiced for outward gain must be transformed into true virtues that are found in wholeness or relationship with the intelligible form and the One.

Wholeness required virtue for Jung as well as for Plato. Jung (1970a, 344) remarked, "Wholeness requires for its evidence a more highly differentiated consciousness, thoughtfulness, reflection, responsibility, and sundry other virtues." The highest achievement of both philosophy and individuation involve the possession of virtues bestowed by grace, "Namely faith, hope, love, and understanding" (1969b, 331). A man who has achieved these attributes is a man of wisdom in Plato's philosophy and in Jung that person is one who has realized "the very perfection of individuality, the ideal type of its species" (1966, 297). It is somewhat difficult to grasp, that achieving the ideal form of one's species refers to achieving ones potential or individuality in dual-unity with the divine Self or God, as Christ did. Christ was the ultimate man of wisdom.

Growing into wholeness through contact with higher being in the soul means thinking, feeling, sensation, and action become increasingly harmonious and providential for a person, because these experiences are a reflection of the unity and harmony in the One or Self. Being correct or right refers to what is needed to afford the most propitious end. "Right action comes from right thinking" (Jung 1966, 226), meaning thinking and acting from a more integrated position creates more harmonious effects, while action stemming from a more frag-mented and reactive pattern result in more difficult or conflicted outcomes. Plato's philosophy also includes learning to think and act from virtue, which also comes from and creates harmony. The wise man who has learned virtue lives according to providence, where events are synchronistically fitted to the path of an individual's destiny.

In philosophy, increasing virtue means transforming knowledge from illusion to wisdom. In Jung's individuation, knowledge moves from ego's instinct and projection where the functions of thinking, sensation, feeling and intuition are out of balance and split into the unconscious inferior and more conscious superior functions, toward intuition, which is the highest, most integrated level of being and knowledge. Intuition according to Jung affords a person the capacity to perceive synchronistic events. Jung refers to Spinoza and Bergson, identifying intuition as "the highest form of knowledge" (1971, 453). This accords with Plato, who considered intuition equivalent to the presence of the divine form in consciousness—thereby providing for the immediacy of absolute knowledge.

To conclude this comparison, individuation and philosophy provide a path for realized being and real knowledge through the soul's capacity to mirror the divine. Jung (1970a, 336) referred to the experience of the absolute as "objective facts," transmitted through psychic events. Interior in nature, psychic events shape all understanding of both the outer and inner worlds. They are "images and forms which alone make knowledge of objects possible" (1968a, 57). This comment of Jung's reveals the Platonic roots of individuation in which he acknowledges that images either perceived externally or realized within are forms, as they are in Plato. Both the archetype and form are manifested in images that are objects of knowledge. When made conscious, these images bring deeper divine realities into one's own being.

Chapter Five
Some Considerations for Psychotherapy Based on the Dual-Unity of Soul in the Third

The addition to analytic theory established in this study centers on the nature of the individual self as soul and the individual's dual-unity in the third, which I have shown to be a Platonic principle revealed in Jung's psychology. Psychotherapy centered on developing awareness in soul derives from our analytic knowledge but on a deeper level, from the philosophy of being. Therefore, we need to take both into account when seeking to understand how to conduct a therapy and also how a person heals. A therapist working within this model would benefit from the following philosophical additions to the psychotherapeutic frame that derive from the esoteric methods of working on the self developed by G. I. Gurdjieff and taught by Maurice Nicoll in the five-volume *Psychological Commentaries*.

The Ontological Frame
The Nature of Being

Ontology is a branch of philosophy that concerns itself with the nature of being. I identify the basis of this psychotherapeutic frame as ontological because to ignore the nature of being while attempting to heal being robs the therapeutic enterprise of its strongest asset. Without a joint understanding of the nature of the self, work in therapy has no anchor and no direction. In my introductory meetings with potential patients, when I am learning about presenting problems and informing the patient about how I work, I present my ontological views of human nature and describe why it is important to understand one another in this department, as the entire healing mission rests on this understanding. Generally, I begin by briefly explaining that my theoretical roots are contemporary psychoanalysis and Jungian or Analytical Psychology as well as Family Systems theory, the first two having a developmental emphasis. I go on to explain that I work with both the intrapsychic (the conscious and unconscious relationship) and interpersonal (self to other in the external world) dimensions of experience. I emphasize the importance of the therapeutic relationship, and the nature of the self as including a higher aspect than our usual conscious awareness, which I call the Self, explaining that it is present as both an invisible agent of healing and an inner guide to developing one's own individuality.

I invoke Jung when discussing the Self and its place in the psychology of being. I also highlight individual resolution of particular symptoms and conflicts as resulting from a more integrated and thus higher vantage point of consciousness in soul, distinct from the wounded ego and the ego itself. Clarity around the patient's experience of individual soul eventually emerges in the therapeutic dialogue at appropriate moments, usually in tandem with breakthrough moments of integration, dreams, or synchronistic experiences. The dual-unity of the individual or soul with the ego and the Self becomes evident to the patient in their own experience as the process of healing proceeds.

It is evident to me that the current trend of considering human experience as epiphenomena of the brain—a view that purports that the beginning and end of being human is the material brain—brings no depth, inspiration, or hope for healing. Nor, in my opinion, does this philosophy of being provide an adequate explanation of change and growth. The anchor for successful work must be sunk deeply into the spiritual ground of being in order to provide ballast for the storms of emotion that arise on the surface. Holding this anchor in one's own being as the therapist, and opening a space in the patient's experience for this deeper understanding of their own process, has a positive effect on the progress of therapy. It brings a patient beyond the wounds that organized their experience into a feeling and understanding of their own self-structure. I have found it expedient and helpful to share my therapeutic viewpoint and method with a patient early in the process since it is well known that a therapist's values cannot be dismissed in psychotherapy. Sorting out whether therapist and patient are well suited at the beginning saves a lot of time and effort as a poor match usually results in no change in the patient.

As I have described, Plato and Jung both include higher realms (the One, the Self) in the macro and micro realms and also show how the macro-universe is mirrored in the micro-world of the human psyche. Both men attempt to address the ultimate cause and underlying realities hidden within appearances, asserting that divine being is the ground of individual consciousness. For those practicing Jungian-orientated therapies, this divine being is the Self. For the Platonic Jung I am presenting here, divine being plays a larger role than usual because acknowledging the soul as the true individual brings in the dual-unity of divine being with individual being. Openly addressing the nature of individual being as divine in the frame of psychotherapy practice is not typical. My own Jungian analyst did not overtly identify the nature of being in our long working relationship. In my experience over 35 years of practice, a philosophy of being rarely emerges in the course of psychotherapy.

The direction and progress of therapy based upon a well-defined sense of the different levels of being is naturally upward. It moves towards integration and a more holistic trust in one's own process, since this trust is founded on knowledge and experience of higher being that is found within the Self. Dialogue about the nature of being in therapy takes place without religious dogma of any kind, being situated within a psychological and philosophical model.

I begin this discussion on the practice of psychotherapy with the frame because it is what defines the field of action of a psychotherapeutic process. As you are probably aware, frame includes many issues on practical and theoretical levels. For example, on a practical level, appointment time is a frame issue. On a more abstract plane, specific interventions, the content of interpretation, and the types of therapist disclosure utilized may or may not belong in the frame one is using. Frame is another way of talking about boundaries, what is in and what is outside of a properly conducted psychotherapy. As I said previously, it seems that most therapists do not start with presenting the patient with an ontological perspective in describing or discussing their therapeutic frame, along with the other salient points about the work that is to be undertaken.

Transformation

Therapy depends on transformation, so the therapist's understanding of the source of transformation should be included in the frame. For Jung, the source of this transformative power is the transcendent function and the dual-unity that emerges through it at the center of being—this is where the individual consciousness is born. This model of the self asserts that behind all transformation there is a higher being at work, and unless we look to it, our minds are shut and we are prone to look downward, remaining in the ego or in even lower states more akin to our animal nature.

But how does transformation occur? Becoming conscious occurs metaphysically while connections are being made in the brain (see the earlier discussion in Chapter 4). The psychic connection that brings two opposing aspects together in the ego remains in the whole or third, where the two have been unified, and where higher consciousness is mirrored. Brain science is catapulting us forward informing us about child development and how affect is regulated, but I am not aware of any science that can adequately explain how substantive change occurs in a person's sense of self or being.

It is left to philosophy to help us understand these deeper realities, and Jung relied heavily on Plato in formulating his psychology to meet this need. Being becomes more of what it was as transformation and change occur. Unity happens on a level of being that encompasses more life, and more depth than the complexes and the ego can contain. This consciousness does not happen, in my experience, in the material brain.

More qualitative then quantitative, being is hard to measure and can only be experienced. Higher being has a radiant quality expressed in attributes such as acceptance, compassion, discernment, and understanding. In my experience, higher being is a substance, not an empty nothing or an abstract idea. I assert in this project, along with Plato and Jung that the substance of being or consciousness is the source of all change and becoming, and that being is the root of becoming. In order to further the patient's becoming, the therapist must develop his or her own being into a level of subtlety that produces consciousness of soul, and then he or she can illuminate the dual-unity of being and becoming for, and within, the patient.

As Plato and Jung asserted, all being is both different as well as the same and the metaphysical and ontological reality of God or Self as a unifying One underlies the many distinct beings. This dynamic (of difference held in the One) means that a therapist can rely on a frame that is constant and ultimately supportive because it rests in the One or Self, the fundamental root of all phenomenon, knowledge, and being. A frame based on being provides a permanent and unchanging basis for trusting all experience in the therapeutic work since such a frame is derived from the One or Self and it is impossible to fall out of being in the One or Self. As complexes are examined in the work, the patient and therapist distinguish what is ego (awareness of a part or one level) and what is true individuality in soul (awareness of the levels of being)—soul being a unique spark of the Divine One informing the biological mechanism and the lower levels.

Relying on a frame of being also means trusting that the supplies needed for healing are available from the higher self or soul of the therapist and the patient. The forces that act in healing, for example strength, understanding, and love, are released by developing conscious attention, which generates love and trust in the relationship with the higher self and the therapist. Pharmacology can assist in mediating a person's comfort level and therefore may be important, but it will never provide the supplies needed for the most thorough healing—this belongs to the realm of being.

The Vertical Axis

In Relation to the Horizontal Axis

The vertical axis is a way of understanding the ontological reality of levels of being. In esoteric Christianity—the inner school of transformation in Christianity versus the exoteric or outer dogma of the church—the vertical axis is found in the universal symbol of the cross. The cross places the vertical axis of being in relation to the horizontal axis, or time and the temporal life. Being on the vertical axis stretches upward from mineral, plant, and animal, to ego, individual soul, and then upwards further to the exalted beings and divine life of the One or Self. All people experience linear time at the point where the vertical and horizontal dimensions intersect, which is the present moment. The experience of other worlds beyond our temporal frame becomes possible as a person achieves conscious presence on the vertical axis.

The ego-self or the conscious point of attention located on the horizontal axis progresses in a linear fashion through time. When healing occurs in psychotherapy, the conscious point of attention transcends up the vertical axis of being, from awareness in the ego and complexes in linear time, to awareness in soul and then of higher realms. Ordinary reality and normal consciousness is ego consciousness on the horizontal axis. Gaining consciousness on the vertical pole expands a person's awareness into the third or soul. With consciousness in soul, the individual is able to apprehend the ego below and the divine above.

Although mostly unrecognized, our developmental, dynamic formulations of defense and symptom translate into an assessment of consciousness on the vertical axis because the degree of self-reflective coherent unity achieved within, mirrors the integration necessary for consciousness on the vertical axis in soul. Soul is always the core of being human but achieving a stable consciousness in soul is a healing act that can also be considered evolutionary because as an interior process, it transforms a person's psychology to a higher state, whereas participating in the outward forms of religion usually does not. By unifying conflict and transforming defensive armoring a person's consciousness ascends up the vertical axis, but every clinician needs to start with a diagnostic formulation of their patient.

Moving up the vertical axis is a unifying of consciousness, and healing can be considered a unifying of consciousness. It is where splits come together between parts of self: thinking, feeling, sensation, and spirit. Traumatic experience is recollected and reclaimed, and the patient learns to relate to their traumatic experiences with compassion, acceptance, and newfound strength that translates into self acceptance. When divisions in the self are reduced and awareness is transformed, experience of self transforms. The energetic investment needed to keep symptoms, defenses, and all their associated mental representations working is redirected in the process of healing thereby heralding change and new experience. Gurdjieff refers to the workings of the average self as a machine, and I apply that idea here to help us understand the experience of the wounded self or ego. Developing the capacity to see or witness one's own wounds and defensive structure and to see the acquired nature of the ego itself heralds the withdrawal of energy from those structures. This transformative act means some degree of freedom from the power of the machine. Freedom is consciousness lifted up the vertical axis.

Since higher being in soul (higher consciousness) is the agent of transformation, placing one's attention—which is sourced in soul but experienced in ego—upon a mental representation or complex produces an alchemical or energetic reaction, as Jung pointed out. This is the work of the transcendent function, which we discussed in an earlier chapter. A conflict in the lower complex is unified through the transcendent function, transforming energy and consciousness up the vertical axis into the third, or awareness in soul. Soul, unconscious or awake, always lies above us on the vertical axis and yet at the same time operates within us.

The vertical axis can be seen as levels of mind or intelligence, with intuition being at the highest level. Symbolic or abstract reasoning is one step down from intuition and linear logic and concrete thinking belong to the sensory mind in the physical world and horizontal axis of time. The idea of level here does not include an evaluative frame nor a value judgment since all levels are their own good and are important to the whole. Nevertheless, awareness of the whole holds more value for human experience than awareness of a only a part. The vertical axis can also be understood as a ray of being composed of finer and coarser energies, called Hydrogens in Nicoll's (1957c, 1103) *Psychological Commentaries* on the Gurdjieff work. This perspective encompasses a spectrum of energies and their properties. We know that some energy, like X-ray, is finer than colored light and such invisible rays pass through the body easily. Finer and finer energies exist as one moves up the vertical axis. When these energies are consciously matched or mirrored in the human subtle body, corresponding worlds open up to human consciousness.

These ever-finer worlds can be thought of as forms of light as well as energy, descending from pure light to denser opaque forms of darkness. Human consciousness stretched out vertically brings light, unity, and harmony into experience. This is seen in esoteric Christianity as the in-breaking of Christ's resurrection or Christ consciousness emerging into lower levels of reality, which is the emerging of heaven on Earth. The vertical axis understood as levels of mind, energy, and light can also be thought of as manifesting different qualities of meaning. Meaning descends from ultimate meaning in the divine into different kinds and qualities of meaning. The level upon which a person is conscious will determine the meaning he or she derives from life, and this meaning changes as level of being on the vertical axis changes.

On the sensory and concrete level of the vertical axis, a person's meaning is most likely organized by the opposites that comprise the complexes, qualities of self-love (an absorption in the self that goes beyond healthy care of one's own needs), and love for external and material things rather than inner experience. On a symbolic or higher level of the vertical axis, the symbol comprises meaning that is synthesized from many things, and opposites are by degree, united. On a still higher level of the vertical axis intuition appears, and here significant degrees of unity are experienced. The capacity to love changes quality as consciousness moves up the vertical axis because the realization that we are all One or part of a unity, as well as separate and different, creates compassion and universal love. The Greeks called this love *agape*. This love for others interferes with self-absorption. These various transformations occur as consciousness extends up the vertical axis, radically altering one's perception of self and world.

Nicoll (1957a, 318) describes this translation of meaning according to level of being in the *Commentaries* of the Gurdjieff work when he says, "Your being attracts your life." Where a person's consciousness exists on the vertical axis determines how they perceive and experience their personal world or their life. The energies of consciousness attract in magnetic-like fashion the same qualities in other people and events. Personal qualities or attributes radiate in many forms in and around a person. The dynamic idea of the repetition compulsion occurs when a person has attributes and qualities that are traumatically based, and these attributes and qualities continue to repeat, translating the same meaning over and over again as time goes on. Moving consciousness up the vertical axis through healing, one is freed from childhood traumatic patterns that are the habitual source of reactions in relationship. What used to be personal attributes, qualities, defenses, and reactions to pain and trauma no longer organize experience. They are always a memory and may recur when a person is vulnerable and under stress. In this case, someone who has sufficiently healed and therefore has supportive resources within their life circle can turn to those in the circle for solace and comfort when challenged by old patterns.

Healing Wounds

Throughout life, a person's quality of understanding and knowledge translates into perception. This is something that happens externally on the horizontal axis of temporal life, and internally on the vertical axis. In other words, what appears in reality is interpreted individually according to a person's level of being. Level of being on the vertical axis is formally identified by Nicoll (1960a, 1267) from the lowest to highest in the following sequence: false personality àpersonality àessenceàReal IàGod. I identify the false personality as the false self, a defense protecting the wounded or traumatized ego. Even further, the false personality can be equated to the Jungian persona complex or idealized self that shows just one side of the self. False self and the persona are more distant from soul than the healthier ego that has been burdened with less shame and is therefore less defensive. Shame and the need to defend create a stronger need to identify with the persona.

Significantly wounded parts of the ego are of necessity self-absorbed. Such self-absorption is actually a highly vigilant form of support constructed unconsciously in an effort to protect the hurt self.

Defending the pain of a traumatized self means that one's interior sense of self is often taken up by defensive experience making deeper, authentic experience unavailable. Focusing on protecting the wounded self often keeps consciousness mostly located in externals as the core self is so defended it is inaccessible. Under these circumstances experience is recorded and expressed in opposites through the complexes without a connecting or unifying force.

The wounded ego and false self are part of the personality. I agree with Almaas's (1996) analysis of the entire personality as narcissistically wounded due to the absence of fundamental being (awareness and experience of divine being). This absence occurs in a narrowing of perceptions of the outer world and felt experience of self…since the inner world, especially the defended injuries, remains more unconscious, i.e., diffuse and undefined therefore unavailable for self experience. As the inner world becomes more defined, unified, and understood, Real I emerges as felt self experience in soul. People in today's world usually think of the ego, including the defended false self, as the seat of true individuality without realizing or acknowledging that it is soul that supports the life of the ego. Mental representations or complexes experienced in the ego consist of feeling-toned patterns of reaction that are physical, cognitive (thoughts), and emotional (affect and feeling). These feeling-toned patterns are habituated over time and thus become a familiar sense of "I" in the ego.

Developmental experience combined with what is referred to in the literature as temperament or what I call inborn soul (which in its initial state is located in a complex in the personality) becomes a pattern of self. This pattern is based on many variables. For example, a primary variable is affect regulation, which is the way that raw emotional experience is regulated, managed, and made meaningful within self-experience. Becoming aware of one's own affective regulation or the ways that one organizes emotional experience, and why one is organized in that particular way, comes about through examining one's early developmental experience. This work slowly changes one's feeling of self. As we have seen in previous chapters, being able to put the parts together within one's own being, and being able to understand one's own emotional process, is an indication that one is no longer completely in the emotional process. The space acquired through this healing in the third is a separation from the immediate and direct self-experience of ego on the horizontal axis. The ego experiences an impact as a consequence of the appearance of awareness in soul and this produces changes in perspective of experience along the horizontal axis or in the temporal world.

Traditional theory emphasizes the fact of attachment to the primary care-taking figures in development, which is important. Also important is the fundamental attachment of self to the ultimate other, the divine One or Self. Most people do not link our fundamental attachment to our divine source with our attachment to our physical parent, and are not able to apprehend how what is above is mirrored below, as Heraclitus said in his philosophy. In our natural life, we develop and grow in the security of a relationship with a care-taker other, usually at least one parent. Our ontological attachment or attachment to our source or origin is reflected here below in our attachment to our physical caretakers. The spiritual relationship existing on the vertical axis is reflected on the horizontal axis, in the dimension of time.

When things are going well, our ego grows in the warm embrace of our parents' love. This love, fostered in the relationship, becomes a pattern of self-regard in the ego, generally called self-esteem and is reflected and expressed in a multitude of ways in a person's relationship to himself or herself. When our natural parent fails to take proper care of our needs for secure attachment, the archetypal, original spiritual parent and home are available as a source of sustaining and healing forces. The opportunity to tap into the archetypal, original spiritual parent and home is even more available when made conscious.

Becoming aware of oneself as uniquely loved by our divine source, and the divine power within our own soul, translates into a healing force as well as a source of self-esteem and regard that sustains daily life. Higher awareness on the vertical axis encompasses the natural, affective attachment between child and parent but goes beyond to the spiritual bond that unites the soul with God.

The realization or experience of our original bond with divine being happens in a successful course of psychotherapy. The patient begins with symptoms and problems and in the process of learning about historical trauma and the way that is carried forward into everyday life they become acquainted with the meaning of consciousness and levels of being above the ego. Wounds to the self caused by traumatic developmental experience and alienation from one's own higher being, are essentially narcissistic wounds that produce an empty and/or negative internal experience. Based on this view, one could understand that there are two levels to address in the analytic work: healing our attachment relationship to the internalized natural parent along with all its associated vicissitudes, and the task of developing a sense of trust in our spiritual consciousness and the higher being that is our original home.

Healing wounds in the ego and unifying the ego itself reveals the self and object representations or complexes. These representations of self and other are a shell of organized energy whose center is connected to the soul (Almaas, 1996, 413). Work on the shell, according to Almass—and this accords with my own experience—makes it flexible and transparent, divesting it from defensive, opaque, and constricted matter. As it is divested of the protective energy, the shell becomes open to others in the world and also the real source of its life—soul and divine being. Becoming conscious of individuality or soul occurs slowly while the wounds in the ego are transforming. The therapist teaches the patient to recognize changing self-states and the changing patterns of self in relation to others, which reflect increased consciousness in soul. Unity, peace, harmony, patience, acceptance, prudence, temperance, and understanding are virtues or states of being that are experienced through soul. As learning takes place through incremental repetition and assimilation, and as the patient continually returns to states of soul, he or she will eventually build a more stable awareness on the vertical axis, which always includes the self-states of the ego because of the dynamic of dual-unity.

The degree of realized or conscious soul is mirrored in the development of finer matter in the subtle body. In my experience this is similar to the physical body at least when in proximity to it. The experience of the subtle body refers to subtle and nuanced perception of realities that are not usually apprehended through the five physical senses. Most people have experienced this in the felt perception of a flash of intuition. The capacity to see beyond the physical in clairvoyance, or hear beyond the physical sound limit, or the capacity to learn information through the telepathic method of touching physical items, attests to the perceptive organs of the subtle body. Awareness in soul and the life of the subtle body create a perception of the internal world that corresponds to perception of outer reality through the five senses, and enhances the latter. The inward center of perception is not a defensive state of isolation. It is instead open, fluid, and spontaneous relating to the self, to the outer world, and to others in a way that is securely rooted in the core experience of the internal self.

The establishment of this inner center does not mean one no longer has any needs for other human beings or external life. Needs are natural, easily accepted and expressed. We all need each other for various reasons throughout life. The essential human condition of interrelatedness does not change as awareness in soul is realized. In fact, when soul is realized a person has a much deeper capacity to be connected to others and the world.

An inward center of orientation on the vertical axis is a reversal of typical human experience. Life is less driven by external influences received through the five physical senses on the horizontal axis. Because people are aware of their own private, inner worlds, most believe this inward experience is a stable and secure base. Actually, outer or external events tend to control people much more than an inner certainty and feeling of individual self. The un-individuated person experiences and perceives in the complexes, which produces needs and states that require almost constant maintenance by outer influence. People don't usually turn inward to encounter the self, due to lack of knowledge about the nature of being.

As the work of therapy progresses and the situation shifts, life is experienced as organized and formed more frequently by internal states informing understanding, which are then expressed in actions that reflect those states. It is this action that constitutes actualization, rather than the reactions often motivated by the five senses in relation to an outer event. This is the reversal of magnetic field, where a person becomes more attracted and anchored in the inner world while living fully in the external, temporal world. Nicoll calls this reversal the achievement of magnetic center. It is the capacity to organize life internally with some degree of awareness of soul or real I on the vertical axis. This magnetic center, or internal depth and stability achieved on the vertical axis is mirrored in the power of presence. Building awareness of soul and the finer energies that belong to it, one proceeds up the vertical axis towards experiencing the presence of the divine One or Self.

When people enter a deep analytic therapy because of symptoms and distress, living in conditions—both inner and outer—that repeat wounds acquired in childhood or other traumatic experiences, internal experience can be numb, alienated, disorganized, painful, and/or incomprehensible. These states are generally unconscious. In order to change, the patient must become conscious of these painful inner experiences. The power to change comes from consciousness, and consciousness is exclusively from individual being in soul. As realization and insight develop and change occurs, it is important to acknowledge with the patient that there are real forces on the vertical axis and in higher being that transform life and assist us in making changes. Without some sense of how change occurs, the patient may not be able to understand or envision how emotional and mental illness can transform and become wholeness and health.

Although our world is one of becoming, real transformation on the vertical axis or an increase of Being in consciousness does not happen mechanically on the linear or horizontal plane of time. On the horizontal axis, life continues in an endless round of effort towards pleasure, comfort, convenience, maintaining defenses, meeting the goals of self-esteem, and meeting the responsibilities of life (among other necessities). This round of activity has purpose in that it builds and protects the ego, but eventually a person experiences a need to reach beyond the life of the ego, a sense that there is more. This magnetic sense prompts work on the self. As Jung pointed out, transformation in the transcendent function does not happen along the natural gradient. Without this magnetic sense that there is more to being and life than what is valuable to the ego, it is inevitable that a person will feel stuck, remain self-absorbed, and continue to be controlled by the machine of personality and the materialistic values that are so characteristic of the western world. Suffering, illness, and distress seem to occur in our lives in order to refocus our attention on finding that all-important step into the depth of true being. Without including the vertical axis as part of the ontological frame, there is no sense of how or where one is going in the healing work.

The Unconscious and Conscious Mind

Another element of the ontological frame I consider important for working with the third is based on the Gurdjieff teaching about the average level of consciousness among people. Although this teaching seems overly harsh in its appraisal of the general human population, after many years of working on myself in this esoteric philosophy and in psychotherapy, as well as practicing psychotherapy over a period of thirty-five years while also observing our global social milieu, I consider it the truth.

This truth is that people are not as conscious as they believe themselves to be. As mentioned before, today there is a pervasive belief that consciousness is a result of the biological mechanism: DNA, the nervous system, the endocrine system, the brain and so forth. This almost exclusive orientation with the physical origins of being is reflected in the pervasive use of medications to relieve psychological distress, and also in the unexamined view that everyday waking consciousness is a self-aware state. In fact, most people have false ideas of how aware they are. In the frame I am considering, waking ego-consciousness is seen as a prelude to real consciousness. For example, during the day one is "awake" and at night one is "asleep" in common parlance but in this frame these two states are not as opposed or as complementary as usual. Rather, I concur with Gurdjieff and the Fourth Way philosophy that everyday consciousness is just a few degrees away from the total unconsciousness of night sleep. Plato and Jung concur with this in their supposition that everyday awareness in the complexes and sensible man is a dim reflection of consciousness distant from soul and thus the Self and One. I, like everyone else engaged in deliberate growth, plug away at self-awareness while accepting the unfathomable degree of unconsciousness still to understand. Humility is organic to the process when one takes into account the infinite nature of journeying towards divine unity, and self-awareness is a natural leveler. This journey makes us know on a deep level that we are all ordinary people. Wherever we happen to be on the vertical axis at any moment, a plunge into one's own shadow may be around the corner.

My own experience of being suggests that the brain, rather than being the source of consciousness, is a signal-processing organ that transmits energy and being into the self. Perhaps the brain serves to engineer life within the earthly sphere and thus provide the foundation for transformation to higher consciousness. During the period when a person is mesmerized and therefore ruled by their physical nature, unconsciousness reins. This is true regardless of how creative or successful a person is in the world. I think Jung would assert that real consciousness is the product of work on the self, which goes beyond a blind acceptance of collective norms and beliefs and fantasies about the self. If people were conscious in a real sense our world would be drastically different from what it is now. For example, all people would have what they need to live, and humans would find no need or reason to kill one another for various different reasons. Nicoll (1957b, 718) puts it nicely when he remarks, "People would be more real, genuine, simple, true and good to one another if they were conscious."

Everyday waking consciousness is a kind of hypnotic sleep, a state of fleeting consciousness. One of the illusions of this waking state is a belief that one is actually awake and does not require healing of any kind. Growing up in any particular family requires time and effort to understand the emotional impact that the family milieu and its patterns of relating had upon a person. Working through what needs to be released and embracing what works is a healing act important for conscious living as an adult, and for the successful parenting of one's own children. The typical level of unconsciousness found among people is an alienation from being that is so fundamental it calls for broad measures. One remedy would be public school education about the psychological life including curriculum in high school that would provide for personal work on oneself. All of society would benefit if this work were required before people embarked on having children of their own. Since we require licenses to drive cars and perform professions, it makes no sense to me why such a monumental task as raising a human consciousness should go unattended. Healing work in each person would integrate some degree of unconscious content, reconnect the ego or personal experience with the soul and our collective unity, and thus make a way for a higher degree of consciousness to appear in everyday life. Most people would then have some basis for building interior awareness, and this collective achievement would change our cultural life.

In depth psychology, the unconscious aspect of our experience since birth is considered the container for every lived experience and includes self-structures that organize affects and defenses (big drivers of personality). In Jung's work the unconscious is also considered to be where the archetypal world and the Self exist. This can be called into human experience through intention and effort. The ontological frame that I am discussing here includes these psychological perspectives but shifts the definition of real consciousness by demanding more of it. What has been considered adequate consciousness, i.e., a person is awake, talking, moving, and otherwise appearing to be self-aware, aware of others, and the world is instead considered in this frame to be a state that is mostly unconscious.

What is considered conscious awareness in the frame I am suggesting consists of a person's ability to observe (illuminate), and then work through the significant affective injuries received during childhood thereby providing space for those internal injuries to transform. Developing the capacity to experience the dual-unity of being is then possible. The simultaneous awareness of ego experience and the witness self—a psychological structure that observes an individual's process in a dispassionate manner from what I am asserting is ontologically above the ego in soul—signifies consciousness moving up the vertical axis. This dual-awareness is conscious awareness on both the horizontal and vertical axis of being.

As mentioned earlier in the Jung chapter, consciousness in soul initially resides in the body and complexes as the point of conscious attention. This point of conscious attention has the potential to extend into the darkness of the unconscious and super-conscious because it holds the root of being within it, sourced from above. The point of conscious attention is the core of spiritual individuality, where the "difference" in creation emerges from the "same." It remains trapped in daily sleep until called into waking life through the act of reflection—this is a kind of meta-consciousness where the witness of the ego and complexes occurs. Reflection expands and thus transforms the conscious point of attention into self-knowledge, which eventually integrates conflicts, heals traumas, and develops wholeness and being in soul.

Becoming conscious of all levels of being is an experience of mystical union. Everyone has a higher spiritual self, living in union with the whole. Discovering consciousness in soul creates a finer attunement in perception and experience than what can be perceived through the relatively heavier, darker, chaotic matter of the physical body and its cohort, personality complexes. Soul heals by uniting the patient's being in all its dimensions and providing for a much more responsive vessel for consciousness than the physical body and personality. Inner versions of the five physical senses grow as subtle organs in the subtle body of soul, as being becomes more conscious. The inner senses have new powers of synthesis and discrimination in perception, while intuition, a kind of direct cognition, becomes more prevalent.

Our collective understanding of human psychology must recognize that failure to consider being and its self-organizing teleology in soul on the vertical axis results in a meaningful loss of sensitivity, refine-ment, and overall wellness. Loss of consciousness in soul translates into a devastating blow for human culture and the world because ego consciousness alone is responsible for the various forms of physical and psychic violence that continue to shape civilization. Becoming conscious on the vertical axis lifts experience above those forces that create violence and harm to others.

The Law of Three

All events that occur, outer or inner events, depend on what is referred to in Nicoll (1957a, 110) as the Law of Three. The Law of Three refers to three forces proceeding from divine unity that are the basis for created manifestation: the active force, the passive force, and a third force that brings the active and passive into relationship in order to create manifestation. Life is a series of events on different scales created by energetic forces ordered by the Law of Three. The energetic forces that manifest as one's personal life (inner and outer events) reflect the level of one's being.

This can be obscure especially as bad things happen to good people. The mystery of tragedy and loss is dealt with in the wisdom traditions through the nature of eternal being, which reincarnates or returns to this dimension of physical reality in order to pursue evolution. In this manner the forces of cause and effect that one sets into motion, consciously or unconsciously, can be worked into balance. The teleological law of being that draws all persons towards balance and wholeness accounts for singular forces or events being unleashed into the state of one's current being from earlier lifetimes. These forces are called karmic traces in the Buddhist tradition. In the psychology of the third, the rebirth of the soul prevalent in the wisdom literature of all traditions, including the Christian bible (Jesus was considered a reincarnation of Elijah) is a fundamental truth explaining the injustices of the conditions of this world.

Most people come to psychotherapy because of an inability to change conditions in their life, inner and/or outer, which is reflected in states and actions that remain on one level of being. Suffering, yet unable to make change, patients need awareness of being—a level above ego—in order to initiate change. But why does suffering occur? Following both Plato and Jung in the hypostasis of being from the One or Self, as being descends, it comes under more and more restrictions and limitations. Those who are asleep to their essence in soul and who are awake only on the horizontal axis, are under a level of constriction second only to the animals, plants, and minerals. Constriction is an inward condition of limited patterns of thought, emotion, and behavior. Limits and constrictions are expressed through the experience of opposites as all aspects of reality on the physical plane are brought to life in the structure of opposites. Nicoll (1957c, 1111) remarks in the *Commentaries* that the more irreconcilable opposites are within oneself, the less meanings one has to live by— that the union of opposites is what gives the greatest meaning.

Contradictions and oppositions expressed by the Law of Three as active and passive forces are brought together by a third force which usually does not transform these oppositions onto a higher level of being. Therefore, change does not occur. It is hard to effect change because a state of being organized by the opposites within is not directly known or experienced by a person who is aware only on the ego level. This makes it difficult to generate the third force that will help transform conflict. Instead, the third force is generated from the same level of being that is in need of transformation. This continues the pattern of experience that generates discomfort or distress, which is often experienced as situations and or events going against the self. This discomfort brings with it a demanding need to attend, to develop relationship to the conditions, and to make effort, if one is able. This effort calls forth a search for the third force that will transform conditions.

Third Force

Gurdjieff's Law of Three and the third force that unites the active and passive forces together resembles our analytic tradition as well as Plato's philosophy, all of which conceive of reality as consisting of opposites. These systems unite the two opposites with a third, and the third can ignite transformation up the vertical axis. Esoteric, invisible, spiritual forces (archetypal or form) create personal reality and there-fore personal reality can encompass more than one level. A therapist works with opposing forces within the patient in order to understand conflict, and this understanding helps create the third force that will unite the opposites and lift consciousness up the vertical axis.

Psychotherapy centered on the individual soul as a theoretical base contributes a powerful third force because it is a higher teaching about the nature of the self and world. In considering the conditions of our lives as opposing active and passive forces orchestrated by ourselves, we are rarely conscious of the causes we set into motion and thus we don't understand when the natural consequences of those actions occur. A desire or what one wants is a force. A thought is a force. Things attract and repel according to the force they conduct. Third force from a higher level of Being is needed to unify and transcend all sorts of conflict.

When third force comes from a higher level of Being it manifests a reality that includes but transcends the two active and passive forces and therefore creates change. Soul as third force brings consciousness upward, towards resolution of conflict via the transcendence of opposites. When it comes from the ego level where the conflict originated, things remain the same and nothing changes. If it comes from even lower spheres, deeper destruction ensues. Working towards change in every session, conflict is addressed in all its dimensions.

Third force that is conducted from the level of the ego does not unify nor raise consciousness. Instead, it continues a sequential experience of one opposite and then the other. This is essentially a form of non-resolution that guarantees that consciousness remains completely identified with the ego. It is being totally "in" the one side of the experience, instead of being able to experience both sides of the conflict at once and thereby witness it more dispassionately. In order to do this, therapy must continue again and again to go back to the two sides of the conflict in the patient's experience. A simple example of this is a patient who has separated from his wife in order to discover if issues around infidelity can be successfully worked through. A part of him continues to enjoy contact with his wife but eventually his unmet needs intrude and the dysfunctional pattern repeats such that he grows angry and withdraws. Working to hold the opposite sides of his experience simultaneously—his enjoyment of his wife in pleasurable pursuits and his dissatisfaction of the underlying emptiness in the marriage—would lead him to maintain his boundaries thereby impeding his participation in pleasurable activities with her. By working through the loss that he did not want to feel, the patient can accept his whole experience.

Facing the realities of relationship can only happen by holding the tension of the opposites in awareness. This mastery eventually results in freedom from swinging from one side of the complex to the other. The process of achieving this is centered in the continual observation of each side of the conflict thereby repeatedly increasing the capacity to witness experience, while working through all the associated emotions. Ultimately, conscious attention will reside in the witness self or soul on the vertical axis, and the two sides of the conflict will be resolved with a decision to accept and care for the self in a way that expresses one's deeper core needs, which supports the whole self.

First and second force in the issues our patients bring to therapy can be seen as trauma or emotional injury (first force) and its sequel defense (second force), which keeps a person defended against, i.e., unaware of the trauma. The patient experiences symptom or distress, signaling the conflicted unconscious material and this is expressed in the continuation of past trauma occurring in current feeling, thought, sensation, and action. Third force from the vertical axis or soul is delivered in part through the therapeutic relationship and the therapist's presence. Because of the work the therapist has done to contain and integrate some degree of their own opposites, unified force radiates from their soul. This presence of soul in the therapist creates a deepening of safety in the holding environment, which is translated into a deeper support in a trusting and attuned relationship. The hope, security, and faith of soul's presence sustain a patient through the painful and sometimes terrifying work of therapy.

Resolving conflict through the third force of soul deepens inner perception. Defenses occurring to keep opposites apart not only serve to protect the self, but also shut out deeper experience. A defense is like a net that intends to catch a fish that also drags in many other fishes that are sacrificed in the catch. The many other fishes sacrificed are a metaphor for the many other experiences that a defense blocks out in the course of protecting the self from a recurring trauma. As defenses soften and inner experience expands, connections come alive, allowing a person to experience a spectrum of worlds: the physical world and the ego, the soul between the ego and the divine whole, and some reflection of that divine whole in soul. Soul's healing force creates these connections and then sustains higher consciousness.

To briefly summarize, third force is usually unconsciously precipitated from the horizontal axis forming more repetitive experience on the horizontal axis in time. When third force is invoked from a higher teaching to purposely and consciously transcend the opposites, it comes from higher up on the vertical axis. When third force stems from higher being, it creates consciousness of the in-between state of soul in the individual—this in itself is a form of third force. In psychotherapy, the third force is purposely created in order to increase consciousness and interfere with a person perpetuating experiences at the same level of being.

Edward Edinger, a Jungian analyst, declared that Jungian analysis was a new religious dispensation because it involved higher levels of being beyond the ego and its complex, and brought those higher levels of being into consciousness. This project concurs with Edinger's perspective on Jungian analysis as a spiritual dispensation and goes even further than he did by considering the nature of the individual self as soul in the third. Achieving individual consciousness in the soul is a form of sanctuary where divine life can be experienced and realized. It is important that the therapist achieve some awareness in soul because the internalization of the therapist as a good object and a safe attachment figure eventually translates into self-structure in the patient—including the self-structure of dual-unity in soul. The therapist's presence in soul contributes significantly to the patient's success in effecting a similar change because of the natural influence of higher being on the patient and on the process itself. A therapist should require of him or herself a personal culture of continual work on the self because effort must be made to maintain and increase awareness.

Thought

Another philosophical aspect of the frame used in this model of therapy is about the nature of thought and its relation to being. Thought, which includes affect—because a thought is always connected to a feeling even if one is unaware of it—is considered an objective reality not just epiphenomenon of the brain. In the Law of Three, thought comes to us as an active, passive, or the third linking force and occurs as an inflow of experience. Thought is a force or substance of its own and because of this it has a powerful effect on one's overall state. Nicoll (1957c, 1196) describes it thus: "thoughts visit, like birds, the cage of your mind . . . all sorts of thoughts enter your mind, on different scales, with different being . . . we are as open to violence from within as we are without."

Generally, people think they create their thoughts and that they are their thoughts. Science does not pretend to know how thought is created or transmitted. In the Gurdjieff tradition, thought is a manifestation of a state, and a state is a place located within an internal, spiritual landscape. Dimensions are states of being and these states of being are spiritual places. They exist as manifestations of the trinity of forces cascading from the divine. Thoughts represent or symbolize these forces and they open to us inwardly, like the outer world opens outwardly to us through our physical senses. Each person has a private, inward space and in this space thought and feeling create internal experience, like skeletal muscles create movement in the physical world (Nicoll 1960b, 1579). What we experience in this inner space depends on how much we can enter into, realize, and therefore manage, regulate and organize our inner landscape, as is true in the outer landscape.

The recognition of a state as a place of being within the inner landscape, and a thought as a kind of radiation of that place, can be understood by thinking objectively of the inner world as a kind of psychological country spanning the vertical axis (Nicoll 1957c, 978). In this country, our invisible selves remain almost completely hidden from one another, traveling from one place to another. We put ourselves in these places through the energetic pattern expressed within. These energetic patterns emerge from the injured ego, the healthy ego, or from consciousness in soul which creates a more developed, unified, and healed state. We can't control our internal patterns of energy until we embark on healing work that allows us to integrate and transcend the conflicts and opposing forces within us. This in turn allows us to master and organize our inner world. Sometimes the wheel of life turns and we are put in difficult places that produce certain kinds of energy. I see this as karma, specific events and people we each must come into contact with in order to ascend up our own vertical axis. Sometimes people share a psychological experience. When they feel this unity they are sharing the same inner place. Those who are kindred in some degree occupy the same places and experience or they perceive things similarly, and therefore they often share worldviews, perceptions of events, thoughts, and feelings.

In the following passage Nicoll (1960b) describes thought as objective, inner psychological space.

You can look at your moods as you look at a pond. A pond is an object of sense. It is objective to you. You do not take a pond as yourself. But as long as you are asleep in life, the mechanical slave to yourself, you will take everything that happens within you as being you. This means that your relationship to the inner world of yourself is as undeveloped, as infantile and imbecile as your relationship to the external world would be if you thought a pond or a tree or an elephant was you. (p. 1690)

Such insight seems bizarre to our usual way of relating to our inner world because we do not realize that our inner world is often autonomous, unknown, and mostly diffuse, non-differentiated, and fragmentary. The haze and darkness that we usually take for our inner world and its constant flow of image, thought, and feeling in response to what is happening within or without, is a reflection of our level of being. Wounded people who appear in psychotherapy often experience a higher degree of darkness and chaos than usual. However, by realizing their pain and need, these people come to the soul. They are in a paradoxical way more privileged than those who are not called to a healing process. Many miss their true path because of our contemporary worldview, which devalues the hidden and invisible while emphasizing a preoccupation with comfort, wealth, and power.

The Bipartite Centers

Originally from the Gurdjieff work in Nicoll's *Commentaries* but adapted for my work in psychotherapy, bipartite centers function in the dual-unity of consciousness between the soul and the ego. The lower and higher centers are a different way of describing how the ego and soul function in the dynamic of dual-unity, much as the Law of Three and the third force is another useful way to understand the opposites and how they unite. I include this brief discussion because I believe the philosophy of bipartite centers adds some value beyond our usual analytic thinking in helping us understand what is happening in healing.

The lower centers of the bipartite structure are located in each complex. The higher centers are located in the soul, whether the soul is undeveloped or developed (whether a person is asleep or conscious in soul). Usually a person's consciousness is located mostly in lower centers as soul begins in its undeveloped form in a complex. When some degree of consciousness in soul has occurred, higher centers organize the lower centers in accord with that same degree. This informs experience and organizes the ego. Centers function by recording impressions. Psychological life is determined by impressions coming into consciousness. A personal world does not exist separate from our perceptions, which are translated into impressions. The bipartite centers are where impressions enter human experience, and centers open up to different levels of the vertical axis. Higher influences on the vertical axis enter higher centers in the human psyche, lower influences into the lower centers. The composite types of impressions or influences a person is attracted to serve to define the level of being of that person.

The organizing, patterning, and structuring principle of lower centers depends on higher centers even when there is no awareness of higher life. It is the higher organizing power of soul that coheres experience even in the face of disintegrating forces, like serious mental illness. Even in the face of extreme disorganizing forces fragmenting the ego, there is always a center in soul that remains untouched. From birth onward, the necessary development of the ego relocates the sense of I to the ego from the soul. The degree to which this happens depends on the kinds of adaptations required by the child and the defenses used to protect injuries sustained in the ego. Whatever degree of consciousness remaining in soul from childhood or achieved in soul through healing, will be mirrored in the experience of the ego. One of the rewards of experiencing soul's unity and coherence in higher centers is that the higher meaning of life becomes experience that is near or close and numinous, rather than distant or empty.

As Nicoll describes, acceptance and rejection of impressions in the centers is comparable to the digestion of food where the body sorts out substances and puts each to use while letting go of the waste. Working on centers is about sorting out psychological life, putting impressions where they belong while discarding the impressions that have no use or meaning. Eventually, impressions are laid down in the unifying, finer matter of higher centers. Impressions suited for higher centers become the aim of a person seeking higher consciousness, healing, or spiritual growth.

The power of lower centers to transform impressions is limited. Rather, lower centers record impressions. Once the ego is developed adequately, memory and association and the sense of self in the ego complexes take over and incoming impressions are recorded in a limited and repetitive way. When this happens, people live only in their associations, and their inner life is formed accordingly. This is significant for everyone, but especially for those who have suffered trauma and wounding to the ego. When people no longer experience new impressions, life is taken mechanically. Taking in impressions mechanically describes a state of unconsciousness that occurs in those who have been significantly wounded and those who are in the state of normal waking consciousness. This mechanical, unconscious condition is that of consciousness located in lower centers, in the ego where impressions are recorded without being ordered, unified, and transformed into higher centers.

There are three lower centers expressed through the complexes or lower self. They are the intellectual, emotional, and instinctual/moving centers. The lower centers are called formatory, meaning they require little attention. Akin to the procedural memory of contemporary research, learning in formatory centers is eventually condensed so one can perform automatically, for example when driving a car. Lower centers are obviously critical for being and function best when used for their proper purpose. Due to lack of knowledge and awareness, most people misuse their centers, meaning impressions are laid down in the wrong centers. Internal chaos is the result of impressions laid down in the wrong centers. When chaos dominates inner experience, energy is blocked at the level of ego or at the level of the wounded ego. Because energy is not transformed, experience remains collective and imitative. One can see this in culture through the collective trends that dominate most people's interests and activities, ranging from ideologies and technology to fashion.

Impressions recorded mechanically in lower centers distance a person from soul experience by coloring life with repetitive and ingrained attitudes, reactions, and defenses. The dead, mechanical impressions that are collected and mixed up in lower centers are highly contagious and provoke imagination or illusions and fantasies about self and world. Because the injuries and mechanical dramas of the lower centers rule the ego and therefore culture, the world lives in perpetuated illusion and ego-driven fantasy expressed in such common atrocities as war, the hoarding of wealth, and many other human rights violations. Ego and its defensive structure, being ruled by lower centers, produce these illusions or imagination. The impoverished ego-driven person keeps imagining that self and world are other than they are, often avoiding the present in fantasies of the future or past. Higher imagination is something altogether different, an objective reality accessed only through higher centers, and the force of creativity in life.

A person has two higher centers in soul. We are fully known and transparent to the beings who communicate to us through higher centers. We cannot hear what is constantly given us through these higher centers because we have not developed consciousness in the third or soul, which connects us with the higher beings communicating to us. These two higher centers are called higher emotional center and higher intellectual center. If we could become conscious in these centers we would be penetrated with forms of insight, knowledge, and understanding that would seem extraordinary and contradictory to what we normally experience. Higher centers are always influencing our life through the sleeping soul, which still structures and vitalizes lower centers even though we remain unaware. We experience the regulating power of these centers in the fact that a "healthy" person's inner and outer worlds remain coherent even though they're mostly unconscious, and an "ill" person's inner and outer worlds remain somewhat coherent even though they are held captive to very distorting perceptions and self-structure.

If a person were to suddenly experience an influx of force from higher centers it would intensify inner life a hundredfold. Nicoll (1960a, 1237) refers to this phenomenon as becoming "crystallized." People are mostly conscious on the vertical axis where the horizontal and vertical axes intersect in linear time. This is a place where consciousness is dominated by time and concrete experience. Crystallization would be destructive to consciousness at this level because enough unity has not been achieved to absorb and withstand the power of higher being. Crystallization is the transformation of substance. It occurs only when development has readied us for higher levels of being. Crystallization in our average state would produce hard, not subtle matter. For this reason, although we yearn to grow and transcend our wounds and pain, we are protected from perceiving inwardly or understanding more than we can usefully bear.

All positive, objective emotion comes from higher centers, which are unified. Such emotions do not have an opposite. They are cognitive emotions full of intuitive knowing or presence. This positive, objective, real emotion is a third force that lifts up consciousness, something I discussed earlier in the Law of Three section. This higher emotion is what heals in psychotherapy.

As mentioned earlier, the three lower centers are the intellectual, emotional, and instinctual moving centers. They are the primary structures organizing ordinary consciousness. The instinctual moving center is turned towards the senses and outer world. The intellectual center is the inner center turned towards higher centers. The emotional center is the intermediary mind that connects impressions received from both the inner and outer focused centers. The idea of centers organizing impressions corresponds to Jung's typology by identifying certain dominant trends in the way a person perceives, digests, and understands a world. A person mainly oriented to his or her sensations or biological mechanism uses instinct-moving center to organize experience. Such a person's consciousness is receiving impressions through physical facts, instinct, sensation, motion, sex, eating, drinking, physical pleasure, and comfort. The instinct-moving center is in charge of the biological organism in all its dimensions. A person orientated to feeling perceives and organizes impressions through lower emotional center. Their experience of self is dominated or guided by feelings and reactions. Nicoll considers ordinary emotion mostly negative because it is usually concerned with the ego itself. For example, throughout the day emotion is often generated unconsciously in efforts to maintain the status quo of the ego-self, and especially the wounded ego-self. Self-emotions are often mistaken for positive emotions because they are so narcissistically cathected, or in other words invested in the sense of self.

Emotional center tends to govern intellectual center as feelings are often unconscious and generate cognitive scaffolding that helps interpret reality. For example, a person will construct a world cognitively in order to assimilate it with the unconscious pressure from the hidden emotion. When the emotional center becomes free of the ordinary emotions centered in the ego, which are often generated to keep one's sense of self safe and supported (real support can be experienced only through higher centers), it is free to unite with intellectual center.

People who are oriented towards intellect organize experience through thinking and rationality. Understanding how thinking and feeling are organically linked together is significant in psychotherapy because much work in healing consists in unifying split-off emotions—which are felt in the body—and linking them with thinking in order to create new experience. Negative emotion produced through trauma and the defenses generated to protect that trauma in the ego is usually linked with mechanical thinking about the badness of self. Becoming conscious of these patterns sorts and orders the impressions, links thinking, emotion, and instinct, and eventually extracts the energy from the mechanical impression. The lower centers must be put in some order, and resolution or integration of the conflicts that occur among impressions must be achieved for transformation to occur.

Like Jung's transformation in the transcendent function where soul is experienced through the uniting of opposites in the complexes, experience in higher centers is based on the resolution of opposites and the integration or uniting of lower centers. This integration of lower centers begins with identifying different impressions as intellectual, feeling, or sensation/motion. Becoming conscious of what kinds of impressions make up an experience puts them in the correct center. Properly working intuition, which is the capacity to receive communications from higher centers, emerges upon the integration of the lower centers.

The process of psychotherapy works to develop the lower centers by making their impressions conscious while connecting the opposites and the varied impressions that exist in different centers. This eventually connects the centers themselves and balances them, transforming energy from ego to soul, and then self-experience slowly becomes organized through higher centers in soul. The work of making impressions conscious, or identifying and connecting opposite impressions, occurs by focusing the attention. As I mentioned earlier, the point of attention experienced in the now is the portal of consciousness originating in soul but expressed in the ego. As in Jung, putting one's attention in the now—on experience of a pattern in the lower centers in the ego—transforms the pattern. Practicing with the attention strengthens the force of soul by investing it with increasingly available energy, as energy is transformed from the lower centers.

Placing the energy in the attention and observing the lower center allows a person to perceive in a new way, feel things in a new way, and understand something in a new way because impressions slowly become united in lower centers, and higher centers awaken in soul. When this occurs even simple experiences can register as beautiful, interesting, and moving because new meaning has been reflected through higher centers.

An important part of psychotherapy is the educational aspect of teaching patients about their self-structure, the wounded ego and defenses, the ego, and lower and higher centers, which I also refer to as the lower and higher self or ego and soul. The patient can then understand the process of therapy and the need to intentionally develop their attention and observe their impressions, or what comes into their experience. All people develop their lower centers differently according to their typology. For example, an artist will develop an emotional center differently than a scientist. Developing the lower centers by being attentive and observant of one's own experience leads to putting them in proper working order.

Most people's centers are not working properly, especially when there has been significant wounding to the ego. Centers usually interfere with one another and deal with wrong things. Each has its appropriate function, intellectual center in thought, emotional center in feeling, and moving center in instinct, sensation, and motion. An example of a center working wrongly is emotional thinking, or thinking led by an unconscious emotion rather than uniting thinking and feeling centers by consciously thinking about an emotion one is aware of, or consciously feeling a response to a thought one is aware of. Dancing when thinking about an abstract problem, or lifting a heavy box while feeling resentment can create internal chaos in centers leading to physical injury or other ineffective or painful outcomes. Having centers operating in harmony and in the correct way creates a quiet, calm internal attention towards whatever task is at hand. Most people remain in-between centers because attention remains unfocused and distracted. It is our attention that brings us into a center and eventually unifies centers. Normal consciousness is often a stream of unconscious, mechanical inner talking and fantasy.

Work in the emotional center leads in therapy because the patient usually comes to the therapeutic session in order to correct and relieve emotional symptoms, which often stem from developmental trauma. In these cases of developmental traumas, difficult and painful emotional experience has hindered the proper development of the ego-self. There is a large amount of literature in the analytic and psychoanalytic disciplines addressing developmental trauma and its sequelae in personality, and the role of the therapeutic relationship in making traumatic emotion conscious. Rebuilding the internal relationship of the care-giving other and the self within the experience of the patient depends on the therapeutic relationship. Emotional or affective healing is the cornerstone in healing and leads to integration of all the domains of self-experience: instinct or body, emotion, intellect, and spiritual consciousness. As the mechanical pull of the lower centers is increasingly resisted the patient develops consciousness of dual-unity in soul.

A Few Words about Soul in Childhood

Understanding some fundamental points about soul in childhood, its relationship to the ego and the parent, augments our analytic knowledge about child development. In this model as it is clear by now, soul is accepted as in-born. In the *The Psychological Commentaries on the Teaching of Gurdjieff and Ouspensky,* the soul is identified as the only part of the human being that permanently evolves, but it can only grow in a small way by itself. The ego and its development are needed as a springboard for growth in soul. The unconscious soul needs a form through which it can experience itself. This occurs when the center of gravity passes from soul to ego in the beginning of life, and the child naturally and slowly ceases to be centered in soul. The feeling of soul is thus indirectly felt rather than directly and immediately experienced.

Throughout development and all of life soul remains the ground of being and therefore is closer and more present than "one's breath," to quote the mystics. However, day-by-day, waking perceptions in the infant and child are put into associations in the developing ego and groups of similar associations become mental constructs that influence subsequent experience. Mental constructs, called schemas by Jean Piaget (who researched and wrote extensively about intelligence), congregate in the complexes and are connected through the dynamic of dual-unity with the increasingly unconscious soul. The soul in the center of the complex always provides for the quality of aliveness that people experience when awake. The more degree of soul that is experienced, the more the quality of aliveness is experienced, with the ultimate feeling of aliveness being in the rapture of mystical union.

The schemas within complexes exist in memory but always occur phenomenologically in the present as organizing principles. Although laid down as neurological pathways in the brain, the esoteric viewpoint is that these patterns are ultimately organized by soul, which uses the brain as a tool for existence on the horizontal level of being, or linear time. Complexes and their schemas are acquired through contact with and proximity to the complexes of the parent and other outer in-fluences. The infant soul is naturally attuned to the parent's hidden being or soul, which is usually mostly unconscious in the complex stage of development. This attunement is natural because the infant is spiritually a unity with the parents, as well as being different and separate. The dual-unity of soul and God is replicated here on the physical plane through the dual-unity of mother and infant. Our spiritual reality is based on a dynamic of two and one, and this is mirrored in our earthly existence in the infant and mother as two and one. Winnicott, a British Object Relations theorist, has said that there is no such thing as an infant, only the infant-mother, as the infant cannot survive without the mother. Our life here on Earth depends on unity and becomes consciously differentiated. It is a one and two or dual-unity of being. As consciousness expands, one realizes that every individual is in a relationship of dual-unity with every other individual being because we are all a One, as well as individually different.

The parent's ego self has a complex form and substance according to his or her level of being (unified vs. conflicted, light to dark, heavy to fine, constricted vs. open, etc., as discussed in the section on vertical axis). The degree of unity in the parent's ego is energetically manifest in different qualities of consciousness and supplies the infant with the power for psychic growth. The child uses this energy and the parent's patterns or complexes as the cornerstone of their own development, combined with the infant's own essential soul substance.

Neglected and/or abused children do not develop like children who are cared for because they do not receive the concentrated attention or energetic influx that their more fortunate peers enjoy. Like the flesh developing through intake of nutrition, the infant's psyche develops through the borrowed energetic, psychic substance of the parent. Like the meat of a fruit around a nut or seed, the child's soul is the seed at the center while vitalizing forces are borrowed from the parent and form learned patterns around that core. These forces, which are substance, support and organize the infant's life and become layered over time into the child's ego self, which develops on its own. When an individual enters into healing, he or she eventually separates a felt sense of individual soul from the acquired patterns in the ego by reforming a healthy and secure attachment with the therapist, and resolving and integrating emotional traumas and conflicts acquired in development. As we have seen, work in healing eventually transforms the externally acquired developmental patterns and liberates the patient from symptom and pain in the ego by creating awareness in the third, on the vertical axis.

The characteristics of soul are spiritual and manifest in the very young child as spontaneity, acceptance, joy, natural creativity, aliveness, peace, genuine expression, compassion, and curiosity. These spiritual attributes continue in the experience of the child to the degree they remain present in the parent. Unless the child arrives with enough developed awareness to recognize what is harmful, which some children who come from extremely dysfunctional homes are able to do, and they remain a mystery to our empirical research when they appear much better put together than their siblings, the parent's level of coherence or unity in integration will be significantly mirrored in the child. The more injured and thus alienated from soul the parent is, the more alienated the child will probably be, although it is important to remember that all persons have their own path in life and their own soul-resources.

The ego makes defensive efforts to protect inner experience from the sometimes longstanding and usually unwitting parental attacks on the child's growing sense of self. These attacks, in my clinical experience, are mostly unconscious and due to the parent passing on a version of their own childhood trauma to the next generation. Conflicts in the parent are intrapsychic and interpersonal, meaning both internal to the parent and also in the relationships of each parent. Conflicts always imply a form of defense, which is a shell that shuts out the deeper essential aspects of experience and causes depression, anxiety, personality problems, and other types of pathology. Pathology always includes alienation from the essential soul, and as we have seen even the healthy ego and its patterns are usually alienated from soul to some degree. It is controversial whether or not malignant pathology found in sociopaths (antisocial personality) can be treated due to the extensive and pervasive alienation and injury that has been inflicted upon the developing ego.

One can see the force of soul in the transparent joy and exuberance, the aliveness and immediacy of the infant and very young child's being. Although a child is resilient, after returning again and again to suffering injury, soul is slowly suppressed under reactions and needed adaptations and strategies in relation to attachment figures. A child requires an attuned response from the parent in order to remain connected to their original, spiritual being. Attunement refers to the parent or caretaker's insight into the inner experience of their child, which is then expressed through interaction. Attunement does not interfere with appropriate discipline. An attuned response mirrors the child's internal experience, digests it, and expresses it back to the child in a way that enables them to understand themselves, the other, and the world. Appropriate attunement is not invasive or controlling.

People who become parents are often involved in supporting their own sense of self to a degree that does not allow for an attuned response to their child. In these cases, which are common, children become a narcissistic vehicle supplying a mirror for the parent's experience; the opposite of what should be happening. The attuned mirroring response the parent did not get from their own caregiver, they unconsciously expect from their child. Alice Miller discussed this insight in her book *The Drama of the Gifted Child*. Unconscious parenting patterns are perpetuated through the generations and can usually only be broken by a parent's determination to become conscious. Since no parent can be completely conscious, the best parents are those who are aware of the need to keep working on becoming conscious.

On top of these difficulties, parents usually have very little understanding or education about their own role in their children's development, or child development in general. Recently, I had a well-educated parent in my office remark that her two-and-a-half-year-old was manipulating her and purposely misbehaving. Simple education about her child's cognitive development helped her understand that the child did not have the capacity for the kind of deliberate manipulation she implied. Such a common misunderstanding by a parent is often followed with disapproval and punitive correction, both hostile to the child's experience of self. There is so much confusion and conflicting information about how to care for children, especially very young children, I encourage any parent reading this to adhere to current research on affect regulation and attachment when strategizing about their own situations. In particular, I recommend Dan Siegel's work *The Developing Mind* and his *Parenting from the Inside Out.*

A parent who is working on their own healing and awareness has a better chance at socializing and educating their child in a way that develops a stable and secure connection between the developing ego and the deeper soul experience. The parental challenge of maintaining within their own being, love, value, acceptance, openness, compassion, strength, intelligence, joy, satisfaction, peacefulness, appreciation, patience, empathy, and understanding is difficult when one is usually trying to develop these qualities for oneself at the same time. Many parents have not realized that these qualities need to be developed in themselves in order to cultivate these qualities in their children.

Whether or not a parent can embody these qualities of soul, a child naturally idealizes the parent figure who hopefully supplies each and every necessary thing. This idealization is gradually transformed when the growing child realizes that the parent figure is separate from their experience and also a source of their disappointment. When development proceeds optimally, this ideal love is redirected through the introduction of a spiritual practice of some sort in the child's life. Thus, a higher relationship with a perfect and ideal source begins, and it is patterned after an attuned relationship with the parent. As a result, some degree of conscious dual-unity in soul with both the higher divine and the practical world develops that can influence the developing self.

When family life is problematic and idealization of the caretaker fails in some way, the idealization of the therapist can provide a corrective experience. Since the divine essence within our soul is wholeness and perfection, the human need for idealization is natural. Eventually idealization should be directed towards the higher object rather than remaining with the lower whether it is the idealization of the self or some other significant other, since idealization in adult human relationship usually does not contribute to health and balance.

Everyone comes into the world with his or her own degree of awareness in soul, weaker or stronger. The degree of alienation of the self from the original soul experience is based on the nature and extent of the injuries received during development, and the level of awareness already present in the incarnated soul. As I mentioned in the last section, there is a large psychological literature describing and explaining the intricacies of injury and defense in character development. Some of my favorite thinkers are Siegel, Stern, Kohut, Winnicott, Miller, Kernberg, Masterson and Piaget. These writers contribute to our understanding about human attachment, affect regulation, trauma, self/object representation, ego, defense, and intellectual growth. This knowledge is fundamental for any working therapist. I believe that Jung's Platonically inspired complex psychology and individual self as soul in the third is equally as important for helping any therapist understand the nature of the self, of being, and the process of transformation.

Epilogue

I conclude with a note about my call to write this book, which began in unexpected subtle body experiences when I was a freshman in college, as I described in Chapter One. In keeping with the mysteries of life, I marvel about the fact that I have not had a subtle body excursion since I began writing my dissertation. I defended the dissertation in 2004, and during the next ten years kept at the necessary rewrites—which included significant changes in both scope and content—through both of my parents aging, illness, and eventual departure from this earth, as well as other family demands. At first, I did not notice that I was not having any subtle body experience, being preoccupied with these various events. After my mother's death I realized that my subtle body excursions had ceased.

 I have wondered about the meaning of this change, especially since my spiritual practice has deepened and I continue to work on my psychological life one would think I would deepen and expand my subtle body excursions. Like discerning the meaning of a dream where the unknown remains within each interpretation, the reasons "why" I have been conscious in subtle body states and the reasons why I stopped remain a mystery. In spite of this, I intuitively understand that once I started writing about these experiences, I had no further need of the call. Continuing to trust the path, now that the work is completed, I believe that the book will find it's way to those who will benefit.

I have learned a tremendous amount from Plato and Jung. Being in their company over the years has given me reason to return again and again to my own soul and the divine life that resides within it. I will carry forward from this finish line my relationship with the invisible yet real worlds that are as close to us as we allow, and a conscious effort to unite with the One dwelling in the innermost chamber of my heart.

I include the following quote from Henry Corbin's *Man of Light* (a wonderful monograph on the subtle body) because it illuminates the reality of soul's dual-unity with divine life, and the truth that we each have the power to shape our own experience of being:

> The archetypal [subtle] body is fashioned according to the extent of his knowledge, to his capacity to understand, to his spiritual consciousness, to his moral conduct, for the more developed his spiritual consciousness, the more moral his conduct, the subtler will be his essential body. The subtler this body becomes, the greater also is its magnitude … each of them creates a dwelling place in proportion to the capacity of his spiritual energy; the narrowness of the place, its sordid filth, its dense gloom, the suffering he endures there, are in proportion to his impiety and his dissociation from the One. Nobody can escape from himself, get out of himself, nobody becomes someone other than himself. (Corbin 90, 225)

Excepting the social and political conditions many are forced to live in such as totalitarian regimes, war torn countries, poverty, hunger, disease and polluted and thus unsafe environments, it is the wounds to the self (the ego self) received in childhood that shape the degree of suffering a person endures throughout life. If each human being, especially those in powerful social and political positions, would heal their own traumatic wounds from childhood, it is likely that our society would improve significantly. Alice Miller articulates this so well in her analysis of Hitler's sadistic child abuse and its links to the Holocaust in her book on child-rearing, *For Your Own Good*. Psychological healing is the Way towards alleviating suffering on both the individual and collective level, and this healing, as I have tried to demonstrate, leads to deeper realizations of the nature of being.

I hope this book brings as much light into your understanding as it has mine, and I wish you well.

References

Almaas, A. H. 1986. *Essence.* York Beach, ME: Samuel Weiser, Inc.

Almaas, A. H. 1988. *The Pearl beyond Price, Integration of Personality into Being: An Object Relations Approach.* Berkeley, CA: Diamond Books, Almaas Publications.

Almaas, A. H. 1996. *The Point of Existence, Transformations of Narcissism in Self-Realization.* Berkeley, CA: Diamond Books, Almaas Publications.

Bluck, R. S. 1955. *Plato's Phaedo.* London, England: Routledge, Kegan and Paul Limited.

Corbin, Henry. 1994. *The Man of Light in Iranian Sufism.* New Lebanon, NY: Omega Publications.

Cornford, F. 1975. Plato's cosmology. Indianapolis, IN: Bobbs-Merrill Company.

Edinger, E. 1984. *The Creation of Consciousness.* Toronto, Canada: Inner City Books.

Harman, W., and E. Sahtouris 1998. *Biology Revisioned.* Berkeley, California: North Atlantic Books.

Heisenberg, W. 1958. *The Physicist's Conception of Nature.* Translated by A. Pomerans. New York: Harcourt, Brace.

Jolande, J. 1953. *Psychological Reflections: An Anthology of the Writings of C. G. Jung.* New York: Pantheon Books.

Jung, C. G. 1935. *Psychological Analysis of Nietzsche's Zarathustra.* Princeton, NJ: Princeton University Press.

Jung. C. G. 1966. *Two Essays.* In *The Collected Works of C. G. Jung* (Vol. 7), translated by R. F. C. Hull. Princeton, NJ: Princeton University Press. (Original work published 1953)

Jung, C. G. 1967. *Symbols of Transformation*. In *The Collected Works of C. G. Jung* (Vol. 5), translated by R. F. C. Hull. Princeton NJ: Princeton University Press. (Original work published 1956)

Jung, C. G. 1968a. *The Archetypes and the Collective Unconscious*. In *The Collected Works of C. G. Jung* (Vol. 9), translated by R. F. C. Hull. Princeton, NJ: Princeton University Press. (Original work published 1959)

Jung, C. G. 1968. *Psychology and Alchemy*. In *The Collected Works of C.G. Jung* (Vol. 12), translated by R. F. C. Hull. Princeton, NJ: Princeton University Press. (Original work published 1953)

Jung, C. G. 1969. *Aion*. In *The Collected Works of C. G. Jung* (Vol. 9), translated by R. F. C. Hull. Princeton, NJ: Princeton University Press. (Original work published 1959)

Jung, C. G. 1969. *The Structure and Dynamics of the Psyche*. In *The Collected Works of C. G. Jung* (Vol. 8), translated by R. F. C. Hull. Princeton, NJ: Princeton University Press. (Original work published 1960)

Jung, C. G. 1969. *Psychology and Religion*. In *The Collected Works of C. G. Jung* (Vol. 11), translated by R. F. C. Hull. Princeton, NJ: Princeton University Press. (Original work published 1958)

Jung, C. G. 1970. *Alchemical Studies*. In *The Collected Works of C. G. Jung* (Vol. 13), translated by R. F. C. Hull. Princeton, NJ: Princeton University Press. (Original work published 1967)

Jung, C. G. 1970. *Civilization in Transition*. In *The Collected Works of C. G. Jung* (Vol. 10), translated by R. F. C. Hull. Princeton, NJ: Princeton University Press. (Original work published 1964)

Jung, C. G. 1972. *Psychogenesis of Mental Disease*. In *The Collected Works of C. G. Jung* (Vol. 3), translated by R. F. C. Hull. Princeton, NJ: Princeton University Press. (Original work published 1960)

References

Jung, C. G. 1974. *Psychological Types*. In *The Collected Works of C. G. Jung* (Vol. 6), translated by R. F. C. Hull. Princeton, NJ: Princeton University Press. (Original work published 1971)

Jung, C. G. 1970. *Mysterium Coniunctionis*. In *The Collected Works of C. G. Jung* (Vol. 14), translated by R. F. C. Hull. Princeton, NJ: Princeton University Press.

Jung, C. G. 1980. *Symbolic Life*. In *The Collected Works of C. G. Jung* (Vol. 18), translated by R. F. C. Hull. Princeton, NJ: Princeton University Press. (Original work published 1950)

Kraut, R. E. (ed.). 1992. *The Cambridge Companion to Plato*. Cambridge, England: Cambridge University Press.

Lorenz, Hendrik. 2009. "Ancient Theories of Soul," *Stanford Encyclopedia of Philosophy* (summer), edited by Edward N. Zalta, http://plato.stanford.edu.

Melling, D. 1987. *Understanding Plato*. Oxford, NY: Oxford University Press.

Miller, Alice. 1990. The Drama of the Gifted Child. New York, NY: Basic Books.

Miller, Jeffrey, C. 2004. *The Transcendent Function*. Albany, NY: State University of New York Press.

Monroe, Robert. 1971. *Journeys Out of Body*. Garden City, NY: Anchor Press.

Nicoll, M. 1957a. *The Psychological Commentaries on the Teaching of Gurdjieff and Ouspensky* (Vol. 1). London, England: Vincent Stuart Publishers.

Nicoll, M. 1957b. *The Psychological Commentaries on the Teaching of Gurdjieff and Ouspensky* (Vol. 2). London, England: Vincent Stuart Publishers.

Nicoll, M. 1957c. *The Psychological Commentaries on the Teaching of Gurdjieff and Ouspensky* (Vol. 3). London, England: Vincent Stuart Publishers.

Nicoll, M. 1960a. *The Psychological Commentaries on the Teaching of Gurdjieff and Ouspensky* (Vol. 4). London, England: Vincent Stuart Publishers.

Nicoll, M. 1960b. *The Psychological Commentaries on the Teaching of Gurdjieff and Ouspensky* (Vol. 5). London, England: Vincent Stuart Publishers.

Nicoll, Maurice. 1984. *The New Man*. Boulder, CO: Shambhala.

Otto, R. 1976. *The Idea of the Holy*. London, England: Oxford University Press.

Patterson, R. 1965. *Plato on Immortality*. University Park, PA: Pennsylvania State University Press.

Plato. 1961. *The Collected Dialogues of Plato*. Translated by H. Cairns and E. Hamilton. Princeton, NJ: Princeton University Press.

Plato. 1996. *The Works of Plato* (Vols. 1-5). Translated by Thomas Taylor. Somerset, England: Prometheus Trust.

Raven, J. E. 1965. *Plato's Thought in the Making: A Study of the Development of His Metaphysics*. London, England: Cambridge University Press.

Reese, W. L. 1980. *Dictionary of Philosophy and Religion*. Atlantic Highlands, NJ: Humanities Press.

Robinson, T. M. 1970. *Plato's Psychology*. Toronto, Canada: Toronto University Press.

Rowe, C. J. 1984. *Plato: Philosophers in Context*. Brighton, Sussex England: Harvester Press Publishing Group.

Siegel, Daniel, J. 1999. *The Developing Mind*. New York, New York: The Guilford Press.

References

Siegel, Daniel, J. 2004. *Parenting from the Inside Out*. New York, NY: Penguin Group.

Stern-Gillet, Suzanne, and Kevin Corrigan. 2008. *Reading Ancient Texts: Aristotle and Neoplatonism: Essays in Honor of Denis Obrien*. Brills Studies in Intellectual History: Reading Ancient Texts (book 162). Brill Academic Publishers.

St. Theresa. 1946. *The Complete Works of St. Theresa*. Translated by E. Allison Peers. London, England: Sheed and Ward.

Swedenborg, E. 1688-1772. *Spiritual Experiences 1745-1765* (Vol. I). Translated by D. Odhner. Bryn Athyn, PA.

Taylor, A. E. 1960. *The Mind of Plato*. Ann Arbor, MI: University of Michigan Press.

Underhill, Evelyn. 1960. *Mysticism*. New York: Dutton Books.

Wagner, Ellen, ed. 2001. *Essays on Plato's Psychology*. Lanham, MD: Lexington Books.

Websters II. 1995. *New College Dictionary*. NY: Houghton Mifflin Co.

Index

Index

Index

About the Author

Jane Weldon has been a practicing psycho-therapist for 35 years and continues to be captivated by the mystery and inspiration of the work. Initially trained as a teacher, she taught movement dance for several years for both students and faculty at schools in southern New Hampshire, and for the Monadnock Arts Council. Graduating from Antioch University in New Hampshire in 1983  with a Masters in Counseling, she earned her Ph.D. in Clinical Psychology with a depth perspective from the Pacifica Institute in Santa Barbara, California in 2004.

In her early twenties, Jane lived for three years in an isolated cabin on a small mountain in New Hampshire with no running water or electricity. This formative experience of "chop wood, carry water" on Pudding Hill taught her the virtues of voluntary simplicity, and how to live in a world often lost to depth, silence and inner meaning. In 1983 Jane moved to Charlottesville, Virginia to begin working as a psycho-therapist and still lives there with her husband, Morgan, and dog, Bodhi. Efforts towards simplicity and contemplation continue to be the center of her life.